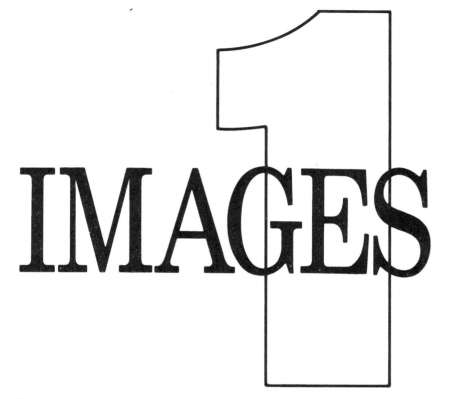

IMAGES 1

English for Beginners

Guenther Zuern

▲▼ Addison-Wesley Publishing Company

Reading, Massachusetts • Menlo Park, California
Don Mills, Ontario • Wokingham, England • Amsterdam • Bonn • Sydney
Singapore • Tokyo • Madrid • Bogota • Santiago • San Juan

A publication of the World Language Division

Dedicated to Heather Marshall

Acknowledgments

Editorial: *Elly Schottman and Kathleen Sands Boehmer*
Manufacturing/Production: *James W. Gibbons*
Photographs: *Guenther Zuern,* except:

   page 61, photo B3—courtesy of the Canadian Imperial Bank of
     Commerce
   page 61, photo B4—courtesy of Canada Post Corporation
   page 81, photos C1, C2—courtesy of Via Rail Canada, Inc.
   page 81, photos D1, D2—courtesy of Air Canada

Photo layout design: *Guenther Zuern*

Illustrations: *Laura Maine* and *Robert Trevor*

Cover design: *Marshall Henrichs*

ISBN 0-201-09804-0
13 14 15 16 17 18 19 20 21 22-AL-96 95 94 93 92 91

TO THE TEACHER

INTRODUCING *IMAGES*

IMAGES 1 & 2: English for Beginners is a visually exciting series for adult and young adult learners of English. Each lesson in *IMAGES* presents a practical, real-life situation through a full-page story sequence of photographs. The photos immediately capture the students' interest and clarify the meaning and context of the language. Each photo presentation is followed by a practice page containing a variety of exercises reinforcing the functions and structures introduced in the lesson and offering opportunities for communicative activities. A Review and Discover section after every six lessons provides additional review as well as vocabulary enrichment. An accompanying tape program offers an integrated listening skills strand.

WHO IS IT FOR?

IMAGES is designed to be equally effective in a variety of learning situations: whole class instruction, individualized instruction in a multi-level classroom, or independent study in a language lab or at home. Vocabulary and structures are presented in a clear, carefully controlled manner. The language in *IMAGES* is spiraled throughout the book for continual review and reinforcement. Each lesson introduces only a select number of new lexical and structural items, carefully integrated with previously introduced material. In this way, the beginning student is able to focus on the functional and communicative aspects of the lesson, and comprehension is optimized.

IMAGES 1 has been particularly developed for the student who has no previous knowledge of English. However, the presentation of language through realistic dialogues and the emphasis on meaningful productive use of all the material presented make this text equally valuable for the false beginner.

HOW DOES IT WORK?

Two questions served as guidelines and criteria for determining the content of *IMAGES*: 1) What do non-English speakers most immediately need to understand and express in order to cope in an English-speaking environment? 2) What is the most direct and natural form in which these language skills can be taught and learned? Functions and notions were selected according to the first criterion. A photographic format, conveying real-life situations through conversations and narratives, was chosen in answer to the second question. Lessons were then developed, linked to a thoughtful structural grading of the material. The resulting program, *IMAGES*, thus offers beginning students unique access to English both from a functional perspective (what they need to understand and express) and from a grammatical perspective (what they need to generate their own language).

Stumbling blocks to comprehension are minimized in *IMAGES* by the gradual introduction of new vocabulary, and the clear conveyance of meaning through the photographs. This facilitates the students' recognition of the structural patterns and rules that are at work. Highlighted excerpts illustrating these rules aid this discovery process. Communicative use of the language is fostered by practice exercises which provide ample opportunity for pair work and role play. The emphasis is on students using grammar to create language that suits their needs.

COMPONENTS OF THE *IMAGES 1* PROGRAM

THE STUDENT BOOK—36 clearly designed and carefully sequenced lessons teach and reinforce a balance of functions and structures through photographic presentations of real-life situations. Written especially for the zero-level beginner, this program is used equally effectively in whole class instruction, individualized instruction, or independent study. An answer key, which can be removed at the teacher's discretion, is provided at the back of the student book.

THE TEACHER'S EDITION—A 16-page guide for the classroom teacher, offering suggestions for expanding and reinforcing each lesson, precedes a full-size reprint of the student book. Many of the suggested activities are designed to promote early communicative use of the language. Texts for the unscripted listening comprehension activities found on the tapes are provided for teachers who wish to incorporate the developmental listening skill strand into their program but do not have access to the tapes.

THE TAPE PROGRAM—Two 60-minute cassettes accompany *IMAGES 1*. The dialogue or narrative from each photo presentation page is recorded in several ways for listening, practice, and role play. In addition, the tapes present an important unscripted listening skills strand. A small illustration on each Review page and at the bottom of every third lesson in the student text reminds the student (and teacher) that a listening comprehension activity is available on the tape. Instructions for responding to these listening activities are very simple and are provided on the tape. Thus, no difficulties are presented for those students using the program independently.

The texts of these *Listening Activities* are provided in the Teacher's Edition.

IMAGES 2, the second level in this beginner's series continues the carefully balanced presentation of English structures and functions. Reading selections increase in length and complexity. Students are exposed to a greater diversity of language, some intended for receptive use only. The focus of the program remains on responding to the immediate language needs of the non-English speaker in an English-speaking environment. As in *IMAGES 1*, the student book, the tape program, and the Teacher's Edition are carefully designed to make *IMAGES 2* a highly effective course in a variety of teacher-directed or independent learning situations.

HOW TO USE THIS BOOK

Individualized Instruction and Independent Study

IMAGES is ideally suited for use by beginning students in a multi-level classroom, or for independent practice and study in the language lab or at home. The method is simple and easily grasped by a non-English speaking student. Lesson 1 assumes no previous knowledge of English. The visual format makes the mode of progression through the book self-explanatory, and a minimal amount of demonstration will get a student started in the program.

Each lesson opens with a photo presentation introducing the new functions, vocabulary and structures. The student begins by reading the photo presentation and listening to the conversation or narration on the tape cassette. He or she repeats the dialogue lines after the actors, practicing pronunciation and inflection. When comfortable, the student turns to the second page of the lesson, the practice exercises. The following exercise formats are used:

Dictionary. This exercise involves writing down the translation of the key new words introduced in the lesson. Since the meaning of these new words is usually clearly conveyed by the photos, the use of a bilingual dictionary is optional, depending on the student's need for confirmation and reinforcement.

Practice A. This cloze exercise reproduces the lesson text but leaves strategic blanks to be filled in by the student. The photo presentation from the previous page is shown in reduced scale, with the dialogue removed. To correct his or her work, the student simply turns back to the original photo presentation page.

Partners and Dictation Exercises. Two symbols representing the *Partners and Dictation* exercises appear after *Practice A* in each lesson.

In the individualized or independent study approach, the tape serves as the student's partner. In most lessons, the tape instructs the student to assume the role of one of the characters in the photo presentation and role play the dialogue, responding to the taped lines of the other character(s). A dictation of selected sentences from the dialogue is then given on the tape. The student is to write these sentences on a separate piece of paper. By turning the tape off at the given signal, the student can replay any or all of the sentences and control the pace of the dictation.

Practice B, C, and D. Each lesson offers two or three additional writing exercises to reinforce new and recycled material. Answers to the exercises can be checked against the Answer Key provided at the end of the student book.

Listening Activities. A cassette symbol, found at the end of Lessons 3, 9, 15, 21, 27 and 33, and on all Review pages, alerts the student to the fact that a *Listening Activity* is provided on the tape. Responses to the *Listening Activities* on the Review pages are to be written in the spaces provided in the student book. Responses to the *Listening Activities* at the end of the other lessons are to be written on a separate piece of paper. The answers to all the *Listening Activities* are included in the Answer Key.

Whole Class or Teacher-Directed Instruction

The following is a suggested method for presenting each lesson in *IMAGES 1* in a whole class or teacher-directed situation. Feel free to adapt and vary the presentation according to the needs of your class and your own teaching style. The Teacher's Edition provides suggestions for large and small-group activities designed to expand and reinforce each lesson and to enhance the communicative potential of classroom instruction.

1. Play the tape or read the photo presentation aloud two or three times while students read along in their books. This provides the students with an initial pronunciation model. The photographs help clarify the meaning and the context of the text.

2. Allow time for students to read the photo presentation on their own. Students may ask each other questions, translate, refer to dictionaries, or do whatever they feel is necessary to comprehend the material. Encourage students to ask you questions as well, and to request repetition of sentences that are confusing or difficult. A student may request a specific sentence by referring to the photo number: "Please read number two."

3. Play the tape or read the photo presentation aloud again. Students then repeat each dialogue line, either chorally and/or individually. The tape

will often then instruct the students to assume the role and read the lines of one character in the dialogue.

4. The students turn to the practice page. The *Dictionary* exercise provides space for students to jot down notes on the meaning and/or pronunciation of key new words and phrases in the text. *Practice A,* a cloze exercise of the lesson text, may be completed in the manner you stipulate, or in the way each student finds personally most effective. The student can choose to correct after each blank or at the end of the exercise.

5. When all students have completed step 4, ask them to cover the *Practice A* dialogue with a sheet of paper, leaving the photo reduction visible as a reference. Write the lesson dialogue on the chalkboard, encouraging students to prompt you at the beginning of each line. Gradually erase key words, asking students to recall and provide the missing words as they read the lines aloud. Continue erasing key words and rehearsing the dialogue until most students can play the individual roles from memory, or with only a few written cues. At this point, encourage students to act out the roles with appropriate gestures. You may wish to demonstrate and facilitate this process by performing the dialogue yourself with a capable student volunteer.

6. *Partners and Dictation Exercises.* These two symbols, appearing below *Practice A* in each lesson, represent the *Partners and Dictation* exercises. Students practice the dialogue with a partner, taking turns playing each role. Encourage students to read with appropriate expression and gestures. If you wish, role playing may be repeated with new partners. Dictation of selected lines from the dialogue is provided on the tape. If you do not own the tapes, but wish to provide a dictation activity, select and dictate 3–5 sentences of your choice from the lesson presentation. Students are to write the sentences on a separate piece of paper.

7. *Practice B, C, and D.* These exercises are most effectively completed as pair work. Most exercises are designed to be done first orally and then in writing as reinforcement of the oral production. Some exercises are intended for writing practice only in order to reinforce the lexical or structural priorities of the lesson. Encourage partners to discuss and compare their answers and to assist each other with problems.

8. *Listening Activities.* Indicated by a cassette symbol in every Review Lesson and at the end of Lessons 3, 9, 15, 21, 27, and 33, these taped activities provide a variety of skill-building exercises focusing on auditory discrimination and aural comprehension. The scripts of the *Listening Activities* are provided in the Teacher's Edition for teachers who do not own the tapes but wish to construct their own version of the listening skill strand.

Expanding and Reinforcing the Lessons

The photo skits can provide the basis for many creative activities. For example, a student can read a line of dialogue aloud, requiring the class or a partner to call out the number of the corresponding photo. New dialogues appropriate to the photos can be created by the class, small groups or student pairs. You and your class can modify and personalize the dialogues by substituting students' names and making any other changes that make the text more relevant to the classroom situation. Depending on the skill level of the group, you can choose to introduce synonymous lines of dialogue which demonstrate different levels of formality or structural complexity. The Teacher's Edition provides many additional suggestions for expanding, varying, and reinforcing each lesson; choose those suggestions best suited to the interests, skill level, strengths and weaknesses of your students, and modify them as needed.

TABLE OF CONTENTS

LESSON		FUNCTIONS AND STRUCTURES
25	I like . . .	Ask/Talk about likes and dislikes; give your reason for something; simple present: *have, want, like.*
26	I need a doctor.	Express necessity; imperative; places: *hospital, bank.*
27	Where is. . . ?	Ask for/Give street directions; question: *Where* + simple present.
28	What time is it?	Ask for/Give the time; ask/talk about personal routine; time phrases: *in the morning, at night . . .*
29	Taxi.	Places in the city; questions: *Where/Why* + simple present; adverb phrases of time and place.
30	I eat a lot.	Ask/Talk about meals and food; question: *What* + simple present.
	Review and Discover	Review lessons 25–30; listening comprehension; street directions; places.
31	Money.	Ask for/Talk about prices; questions: *How much* + *to be*/simple present.
32	How much is. . . ?	Identify/Ask for prices of specific items; *these/those*; object pronouns: *I'll take it/them.*
33	That's too expensive.	Compare prices; request/identify items in a store; question: *Which* + *to be.*
34	Restaurant.	Make requests/Order food in a restaurant.
35	I want to go to. . . .	Ask for information about public transportation; *want* + infinitive; *there is . . .*
36	English is easy.	Express capability/incapability; modal: *can* + verb; Imperative: *Don't. . . .*
	Review and Discover	Review lessons 31–36; listening comprehension; stores and their products; request change for coins and bills.

Hello.

Practice ————————

My name is ————————————

My first name is ————————————

My last name is ————————————

————————————
Signature

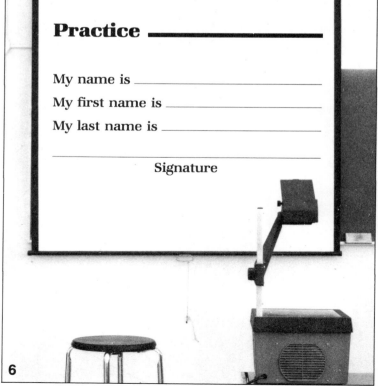

2

How are you?

☞ What's = What is

Dictionary

first _____	name _____
is _____	what _____
last _____	your _____
my _____	

Practice A

[★ Hello.

[★ My _____*name*_____ is David Benson.

[★ My _____ name is David.

[★ My _____ name is Benson.

[★ What's your _____ ?

Dictionary

and _____	how _____
are _____	thanks _____
fine _____	you _____

Practice B

[★ _____*Hello*_____ , Anna.

[○ Hello, David. How _____ _____ ?

[★ _____ , thanks. And you?

[○ Fine.

Practice C

are, is, first, <u>name</u>, thanks, last, you

1. ★ What's your _____*name*_____ ?

   ○ Tom Lee.

   ★ My name _____ David Benson.

   ○ How _____ you, David?

   ★ Fine, _____ . And _____ ?

   ○ Fine.

2. ★ What's your _____ name?

   ○ Anna.

   ★ What's your _____ name?

   ○ Morgan.

Pardon?

5

you're = you are   thanks = thank you

Dictionary

here _____

pardon _____

please _____

welcome _____

Practice A

[★ What's your _name_____ ?
[○ Tony Santos.

[★ Spell _____ last name, please.
[○ _____ ?

[★ Spell _____ last name.
[○ Ahh! S-A-N-T-O-S.

[★ Sign here, _____ .

[★ _____ you.
[○ You're_____ .

Practice B

1. How are you?
_____

2. What's your name?
_____

3. Spell your first name, please.
_____

4. Spell your last name.
_____

5. Sign here please.
_____

Practice C

1. ★ _What's your name_____?
   ○ Anna Morgan.

2. ★ _____?
   ○ Fine, thanks.

3. ★ _____.
   ○ M-O-R-G-A-N.

4. ★ _____.
   ○ A-N-N-A.

5. ★ _____.
   ○ You're welcome.

Nice to meet you.

👉 Hi = Hello   Bye = Good-bye   Mr. = Mister

David, this is Mr. Lee.

Nice to meet you, Mr. Lee.   Nice to meet you, too.

Dictionary

good _____   Mrs. _____

good-bye _____   Ms. _____

meet _____   nice _____

Miss _____   this _____

Mr. _____   too _____

Practice A

[★ Hi, Susan.

[○ Hi, Ken. How _are_ _____ ?

[★ _____ .

[○ Ken, _____ is Lisa.

[★ Nice to _____ you.

[■ Nice to _____ you, _____ .

[★ Good-bye, Susan.

[○ _____ .

[★ _____ , Lisa.

[■ Bye, Ken.

Practice B

1. ★ Spell _____ first name, _____ .

   ○ T-O-N-Y.

   ★ _____ you.

   ○ You're _____ .

2. ★ David, this _____ Mr. Lee.

   ○ Nice to meet _____ , Mr. Lee.

   ★ Nice to meet _____ , _____ .

3. ★ Hello, Anna. _____ are you?

   ○ _____ , thanks. _____ you?

   ★ _____ .

Practice C

1. name / last / Spell / your
   Spell your last name _____ .

2. Nice / meet / to / you

   _____ .

3. My / name / last / Benson / is

   _____ .

4. you / How / are

   _____ ?

5. name / first / your / What's

   _____ ?

I am a teacher.

I am a teacher.

This is Tony. He is a student.

This is Maria. She is a student, too.

They are students in my English class.

We are students.

You are a teacher.

Yes, and you are very good students.

☞ 1 student   2, 3 . . . student<u>s</u>

Dictionary

I am_____	We are_____
He is _____	You are _____
She is _____	They are _____
a _____	teacher _____
class _____	very _____
in _____	yes _____
student _____	

Practice A

[★ I _am_____ a teacher.
[★ This _____ Tony. He _____ a student.
[★ This _____ Maria. She _____ a student, too.
[★ They _____ students in my English class.
[○ We _____ students.
[○ You _____ a teacher.
[★ Yes, and you _____ very good students.

Practice B

I, you, he, she, we, they

1. Tony and I are students.
   _We_____ are students.
2. Tony and Maria are students.
   _____ are students.
3. David Benson is a teacher.
   _____ is a teacher.
4. Maria is a student.
   _____ is a student.
5. Maria and I are students.
   _____ are students.
6. Tony and Maria are in my English class.
   _____ are in my English class.
7. Tom Lee is a teacher, too.
   _____ is a teacher, too.
8. _____ am a student.
9. _____ are a teacher.

Practice C

am, is, are

1. My name _is_____ David Benson.
2. I _____ David Benson.
3. How _____ you?
4. This _____ Mr. Lee.
5. They _____ students.
6. We _____ students.
7. He _____ a good teacher.
8. You _____ good students.
9. She _____ in my English class.
10. Mr. Benson _____ my teacher.
11. Tony and Maria _____ in my class.
12. I _____ a student.
13. You _____ a good student.
14. Tony and Maria _____ good students.
15. What _____ your name?
16. You _____ welcome.

10

I'm, you're, he's . . .

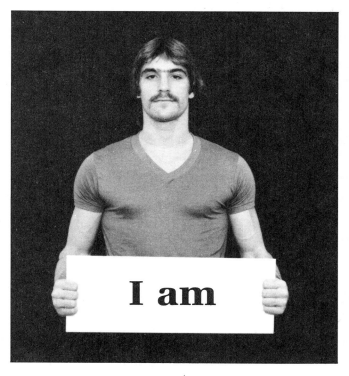

I am	➤	I'm
You are	➤	You're
He is	➤	He's
She is	➤	She's
We are	➤	We're
They are	➤	They're

I'm a student.
You're a student.
He's a student.
She's a student.
We're students.
They're students.

NUMBERS

0	zero				
1	one	11	eleven	21	twenty-one
2	two	12	twelve	22	twenty-two, twenty-three . . . .
3	three	13	thirteen	30	thirty . . . .
4	four	14	fourteen	40	forty . . . .
5	five	15	fifteen	50	fifty . . . .
6	six	16	sixteen	60	sixty . . . .
7	seven	17	seventeen	70	seventy . . . .
8	eight	18	eighteen	80	eighty . . . .
9	nine	19	nineteen	90	ninety . . . . , ninety-nine
10	ten	20	twenty	100	one hundred

Practice A

I am   IIII➡ *I'm*

You are   IIII➡ _____

He is   IIII➡ _____

She is   IIII➡ _____

We are   IIII➡ _____

They are IIII➡ _____

Practice B

[★ *I'm* _____ a teacher.

[★ This is Tony. _____ a student.

[★ This is Maria. _____ a student, too.

[★ _____ students in my English class.

[○ *We're* _____ students.

[○ _____ a teacher.

[★ Yes, and _____ very good students.

Practice C

1. He is a good teacher.
   He's a good teacher.
2. We are students.
   _____
3. You are welcome.
   _____
4. He is in my English class.
   _____
5. She is in my English class, too.
   _____
6. What is your name?
   _____
7. They are teachers.
   _____
8. I am a student.
   _____
9. They are very good students.
   _____

Practice D

(i)

0 *zero*_____

1 _____

2 _____

3 _____

4 _____

5 _____

6 _____

7 _____

8 _____

9 _____

10 _____

(ii)

thirteen   *13*

twenty   _____

eleven   _____

nineteen   _____

sixteen   _____

twelve   _____

fifteen   _____

eighteen   _____

seventeen   _____

fourteen   _____

twenty-one   _____

Excuse me.

Excuse me.

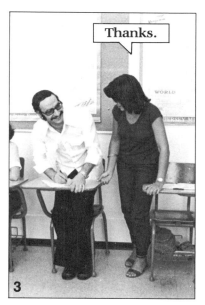

Thanks.

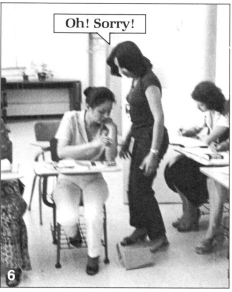

Oh! Sorry!

I'm sorry.

That's OK.

Here is your book.

Thank you.

You're welcome.

that is |||➡ that's

Dictionary

book _____   sorry _____

excuse _____   telephone _____

me _____   that _____

OK _____   this _____

pen _____

Practice A

[★ *Excuse* _____ _____ .

[★ Thanks.

[★ Oh! _____ !

[★ I'm _____ .

[○ That's _____ .

[★ _____ is your book.

[○ Thank you.

[★ You're _____ .

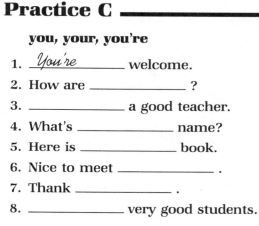

Practice C

you, your, you're

1. *You're* _____ welcome.

2. How are _____ ?

3. _____ a good teacher.

4. What's _____ name?

5. Here is _____ book.

6. Nice to meet _____ .

7. Thank _____ .

8. _____ very good students.

Practice B

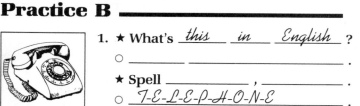

1. ★ What's *this* *in* *English* ?
   ○ _____ _____ .
   ★ Spell _____ , _____ .
   ○ *T-E-L-E-P-H-O-N-E* .

2. ★ What's _____ _____ ?
   ○ _____ _____ .
   ★ Spell _____ , _____ .
   ○ _____ .

3. ★ What's _____ _____ ?
   ○ _____ _____ .
   ★ Spell _____ , _____ .
   ○ _____ .

REVIEW/Lessons 1–6

WHAT'S THE WORD?

1. is ⟨this⟩
2. am   and
3. she   we

4. you   your
5. here   we're
6. he   hi

7. they're   are
8. me   my
9. Miss   Mrs.

YES OR NO?

1. Maria is a student.   ⟨YES⟩   NO
2. Mrs. Kennedy is a student.   YES   NO
3. Mrs. Benson is my English teacher.   YES   NO
4. Mr. Benson is a very good teacher.   YES   NO
5. Tony is a very good teacher, too.   YES   NO
6. Anna is in my English class.   YES   NO
7. Anna and Tony are very good students.   YES   NO
8. Maria is a good student, too.   YES   NO

WHAT'S ONE + ONE?

ACROSS
1. one + one
3. twenty-two + eight
8. thirteen + four
10. thirty-one + nine
11. six + five
12. he is
13. you are

DOWN
2. zero + one
3. seven + five
4. fourteen + six
5. they are
6. one + two
7. four + four
8. she is
9. three + seven
10. two + two

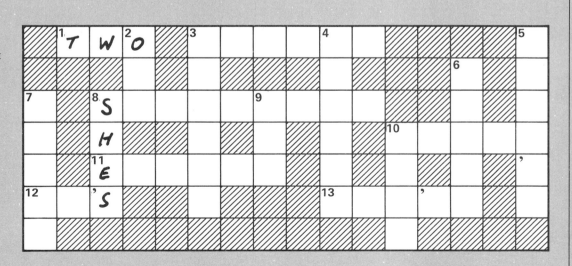

DISCOVER/Lessons 1-6

 bookcase _____

 chair _____

 map _____

 desk _____

 lamp _____

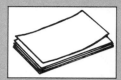 paper _____

 pencil _____

 plant _____

 stapler _____

 typewriter _____

Discover A

1. p a r e p   *paper* _____
2. k s e d   _____
3. t a p l n   _____
4. o o b k s e c a   _____
5. h i r a c   _____
6. p l a m   _____

1. P A P E R
2. ☐ ☐ ☐ ☐
3. ☐ ☐ ☐ ☐ ☐
4. ☐ ☐ ☐ ☐ ☐ ☐ ☐ ☐
5. ☐ ☐ ☐ ☐ ☐
6. ☐ ☐ ☐ ☐

Discover B

1. _____

2. _____

3. _____

4. _____

5. *telephone* _____

6. _____
7. _____
8. _____

16

I'm hungry.

1. I'm hungry.

2. I'm thirsty.

3. I'm tired.

4. I'm hot.

5. I'm cold.

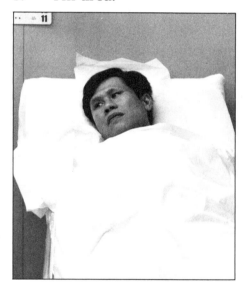

6. I'm sick.

7. I'm happy.

8. I'm unhappy.

9. We're married.

Practice A

1. <u>*I'm hungry.*</u>
2. _____
3. _____
4. _____
5. _____
6. _____
7. _____
8. _____
9. _____

Practice B

[★ What's your <u>*name*</u> ?
[○ Tony Santos.

[★ Spell _____ last name, please.
[○ _____ ?

[★ Spell _____ last name.
[○ Ahh! S-A-N-T-O-S .

[★ Sign here, _____ .

[★ _____ you.
[○ You're _____ .

Practice C

[★ Hi, Susan.

[○ Hi, Ken. How <u>*are*</u> _____ ?
[★ _____ .

[○ Ken, _____ is Lisa.

[★ Nice to _____ you.
[■ Nice to _____ you, _____ .

[★ Good-bye, Susan.
[○ _____ .

[★ _____ , Lisa.
[■ Bye, Ken.

Are you thirsty?

☞ You are hot.　I am thirsty.
Are you hot?　I am <u>not</u> thirsty.　▐▐▐➡ I'm not thirsty.

Dictionary

no _____　so _____

not _____　why _____

Practice A

[★ I'm hot.

[★ <u>*Are*</u> <u>*you*</u> hot?

└ ○ Yes, I am.

[★ I'm thirsty, too.

[★ _____ _____ thirsty?

└ ○ No, I'm not.

[■ Hi.

└ ○ ★ Hi.

[○ _____ are you, Ken?

[■ _____ so good.

[○ _____ ?

[■ I'm hot.

[○ _____ too.

Practice B

1. <u>*Are you thirsty*</u> ? <u>*Yes, I am*</u> .
2. _____ ? _____ .
3. _____ ? _____ .
4. _____ ? _____ .
5. _____ ? _____ .
6. _____ ? _____ .

Practice C

(i) He, She, We, They

1. Susan and Lisa are hot.
   <u>*They are hot.*</u>
2. Ken is unhappy.
   _____
3. Susan is thirsty.
   _____
4. Anna and I are married.
   _____

(ii) am, is, are

1. He <u>*is*</u> hot.
2. She _____ thirsty.
3. I _____ unhappy.
4. We _____ married.
5. They _____ happy.
6. He _____ sick.
7. _____ you a student?

(iii) I, my, me

1. <u>*My*</u> name is David.
2. Excuse _____ .
3. _____ am very tired.
4. _____ too.
5. _____ last name is Lee.
6. _____ am not hungry.
7. _____ name is Tony.

Where are you from?

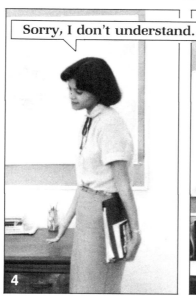

☞ I do not ‖‖➡ I don't

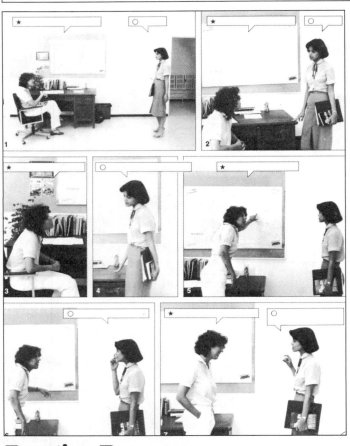

Dictionary

but _____	Spanish _____
from _____	speak _____
little _____	then _____
new _____	understand _____
only _____	where _____

Practice A

[★ _Are_ _____ a new student?
[○ Pardon?

[★ _____ _____ a new student?
[○ Oh, yes.

[★ _____ _____ _____ from?
[○ Sorry, I don't _____ .
[★ _____ _____ _____ from?
[○ Ahh! I'm from Mexico.

[★ Then, you _____ Spanish.
[○ Yes, but I _____ only a _____ English.

Practice B

1. What's your first name?	A telephone.
2. What's this?	Canada.
3. How are you?	Tony.
4. Where are you from?	Yes, I am.
5. Are you hungry?	Santos.
6. What's your last name?	Fine.

Practice C

me, from, speak, not, nice, don't, where, what's

1. _Nice_ _____ to meet you.
2. _____ this?
3. I'm _____ thirsty.
4. I _____ understand.
5. I _____ English and Spanish.
6. _____ are you from?
7. Excuse _____ .
8. I'm _____ Japan.

Practice D

1. ★ I'm tired. _Are you tired_ ? ○ _No, I'm not tired_ .
2. ★ I'm married. _____ ? ○ _____ .
3. ★ I'm a teacher. _____ ? ○ _____ .
4. ★ I'm from Japan. _____ ? ○ _____ .
5. ★ I'm a new student. _____ ? ○ _____ .
6. ★ I'm hungry. _____ ? ○ _____ .

Country, city . . .

A

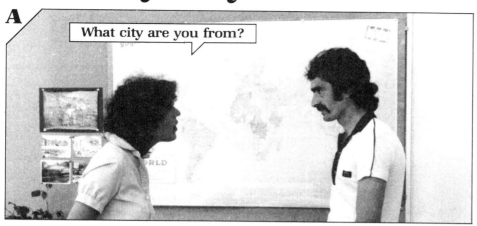

What city are you from?

★ Where are you from?
○ I'm from Brazil.

★ What city are you from?
○ Rio de Janeiro. And you?
Are you from Toronto?

★ No, I'm from Montreal.

B

1

2

Canada is a big country.
Panama is a small country.

3

4

Canada is cold.
Panama is hot.

5

Toronto isn't a small city.
Toronto is a big city.
Toronto is beautiful, too.

Toronto is a big city.
Toronto is <u>not</u> a small city. ⓦ Toronto isn't a small city.

rich

poor

Dictionary

beautiful _____

big _____

city _____

country _____

poor _____

rich _____

small _____

Practice A

A. ★ Where *are* *you* _____ ?

   ○ I'm _____ Brazil.

   ★ _____ _____ are you from?

   ○ Rio de Janeiro. And you?

     Are you from Toronto?

   ★ No, _____ from Montreal.

B. Canada is a *big* country.

   Panama is a _____ country.

   Canada _____ cold.

   Panama _____ _____ .

   Toronto _____ a small city.

   Toronto is a _____ city.

   Toronto is _____ , too.

Practice B

1. _What's your name_ ? David Benson.
2. _____ ? I'm from Mexico.
3. _____ ? I'm from Toronto.
4. _____ ? Fine.
5. _____ ? No, I'm not hot.

Practice C

is, isn't

1. Panama *isn't* a big country.
2. The U.S.A. _____ a big country.
3. Tokyo _____ a small city.
4. Brazil _____ cold.
5. Princess Diana _____ beautiful.

Practice D

1. country / rich / Japan / is / a
   Japan is a rich country .
2. poor / isn't / Canada / a / country
   _____ .
3. small / is / Switzerland
   _____ .
4. is / city / a / big / New York
   _____ .
5. very / cold / is / Alaska
   _____ .
6. a / city / beautiful / is / Paris
   _____ .
7. city / a / very / big / is / Tokyo
   _____ .
8. isn't / cold / Brazil
   _____ .

Sunday, Monday . . .

A

year →	1985	SEPTEMBER			1985	
Sunday	**Monday**	**Tuesday**	**Wednesday**	**Thursday**	**Friday**	**Saturday**
1	2	3	4	5	6	7
8	9	10	11	12	13	14
15	16	17	18	19	20	21
22	23	24	25	26	27	28

year —
month —
day
week —

★ What day is today?
○ Today is Monday.

★ What day is before Monday?
○ Sunday.

★ What day is after Monday?
○ Tuesday.

B

winter

spring

January
February
March
April
May
June
July
August
September
October
November
December

summer

fall

★ What month is this month?
○ This month is September.

★ What month is before September?
○ August.

★ What month is after September?
○ October.

25

1985		SEPTEMBER			1985	
Sunday	Monday	Tuesday	Wednesday	Thursday	Friday	Saturday
1	2	3	4	5	6	7
8	9	10	11	12	13	14
15	16	17	18	19	20	21
22	23	24	25	26	27	28

year _____
_____
_____
_____

1. _____
2. _____
3. _____
4. _____

Dictionary

after _____   today _____

before _____   week _____

day _____   year _____

month _____

Practice A

A. ★ _____ day is today?

○ Today _____ Monday.

★ What day is _____ Monday?

○ Sunday.

★ What day is _____ Monday?

○ Tuesday.

B. ★ _____ month is this month?

○ This _____ is September.

★ What month _____ before September?

○ _____ .

★ _____ _____ is after September?

○ _____ .

Practice B

1. ★ What day is before Wednesday?

   ○ _Tuesday_ .

2. ★ What day is after Sunday?

   ○ _____ .

3. ★ What month is after December?

   ○ _____ .

4. ★ What month is before August?

   ○ _____ .

5. ★ What month is this month?

   ○ _____ .

6. ★ What day is today?

   ○ _____ .

7. ★ What day is after Friday?

   ○ _____ .

8. ★ What day is before Friday?

   ○ _____ .

9. ★ What month is after October?

   ○ _____ .

Practice C

(i)

1. January
2. _February_
3. March
4. _____
5. May
6. _____
7. July
8. _____
9. September
10. _____
11. November
12. _____

(ii)

1. Sunday
2. _Monday_
3. Tuesday
4. _____
5. Thursday
6. _____
7. _____

What's your address?

1. ★ What's your address?
   ○ My address is 145 Church Street.

2. ★ What's your telephone number?
   ○ My telephone number is 961-7721.

3. ★ How old are you?
   ○ I'm twenty-seven.

4. ★ What's your date of birth?
   ○ July 16, 1958.

145 Church Street = One forty-five Church Street.
July 16, 1958 = July sixteenth, nineteen fifty-eight.

Dictionary

address _____

date of birth _____

old _____

street _____

Practice A

1. ★ What's your _____ ?
   ○ My _____ is 145 Church Street.
2. ★ What's your _____ _____ ?
   ○ My _____ _____ is 961-7721.
3. ★ _____ _____ are you?
   ○ I'm twenty-seven.
4. ★ What's your _____ _____ _____ ?
   ○ July 16, 1958.

Practice B

1. *What's your address* ? 275 King Street.
2. _____ ? 961-4765.
3. _____ ? I'm 36.
4. _____ ? May 16, 1949.
5. _____ ? The U.S.A.
6. _____ ? No, I'm not married.
7. _____ ? Yes, I'm from Chicago.
8. _____ ? Fine, thanks.
9. _____ ? David Wong.
10. _____ ? No, I'm not tired.

Practice C

country, city, today, not, don't, little, speak, me, from

1. *Today* _____ is Wednesday.
2. Sorry, I _____ understand.
3. No, I'm _____ hungry.
4. I speak only a _____ English.
5. Japan is a rich _____ .
6. Excuse _____ .
7. I _____ Spanish and English.
8. What _____ are you from?
9. I'm _____ China.

Practice D

1. What's your address? _____ .
2. What's your telephone number? _____ .
3. How old are you? _____ .
4. What's your date of birth? _____ .
5. Where are you from? _____ .
6. What city are you from? _____ .

REVIEW/Lessons 7–12

HOW ARE YOU?

cold, happy, hot, hungry, married, sick, thirsty, tired, unhappy

1. He _is_ _unhappy_ .
2. She _____ _____ .
3. They _____ _____ .

4. I _____ _____ .
5. She _____ _____ .
6. We _____ _____ .

KIM TANAKA

1. My first name is Tanaka.   YES   NO

2. I'm a student.   YES   NO

3. My date of birth is August 6, 1964.   YES   NO

4. I am from Japan.   YES   NO

5. Japan isn't a big country.   YES   NO

6. Tokyo is a small city.   YES   NO

7. Tokyo is a beautiful city.   YES   NO

HOW ABOUT YOU?

1. Are you a new student? _____
2. What's your last name? _____
3. What's your first name? _____
4. Are you married? _____
5. Are you from Mexico? _____
6. Are you from Brazil? _____
7. Are you from a big city? _____
8. What city are you from? _____
9. What day is today? _____
10. What month is this month? _____

DISCOVER/Lessons 7–12

Dictionary

Street ➤ St.		East ➤ E.	
Avenue ➤ Ave.		West ➤ W.	
Road ➤ Rd.		North ➤ N.	
Drive ➤ Dr.		South ➤ S.	
Place ➤ Pl.		Apartment ➤ Apt.	

Discover A

1. 2215 Spears Rd. Apt. 6, Houston
   Twenty-two fifteen Spears Road,
   Apartment six, Houston

2. 849 W. University St. Apt. 1450

3. 734 S. Main Ave. Albany

4. 3518 N. Orange Dr. Los Angeles

5. 62 Washington Pl. Apt. 2832

6. (your address)

Discover B

1st/first	11th/eleventh	21st/twenty-first
2nd/second	12th/twelfth	22nd/twenty-second
3rd/third	13th/thirteenth	23rd/twenty-third
4th/fourth	14th/fourteenth	24th/twenty-fourth
5th/fifth	15th/fifteenth	25th/twenty-fifth
6th/sixth	16th/sixteenth	26th/twenty-sixth
7th/seventh	17th/seventeenth	27th/twenty-seventh
8th/eighth	18th/eighteenth	28th/twenty-eighth
9th/ninth	19th/nineteenth	29th/twenty-ninth
10th/tenth	20th/twentieth	30th/thirtieth

1. May 19, 1973
   May nineteenth, nineteen seventy-three

2. October 27, 1959

3. November 3, 1964

4. June 1, 1935

5. (your birthday)

Discover C

1. 772-6520   Seven-seven-two, six-five-two-oh (zero)

2. _____   Four-two-eight, five thousand

3. _____   Three-four-one, three-oh-five-nine

4. _____
   (your number)

5. _____
   (the fire department)

6. _____
   (the police)

Is this your pen?

A

1. TV (television)

2. radio

3. car

4. jacket

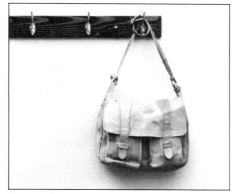

5. bag

6. bicycle

7. It's a house.

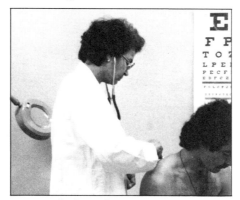

8. She's a doctor.

9. He's a mechanic.

B

1

Is this your pen?

Yes, it is. Thank you.

2

31

 👧 ⟶ She   It is |||➡ It's

👦 ⟶ He

☐ ⟶ It

Practice A

A. 1. What's number one? *It's a TV* .

    2. What's number two? _____ .

    3. What's number three? _____ .

    4. What's number four? _____ .

    5. What's number five? _____ .

    6. What's number six? _____ .

    7. It's a _____ .

    8. She's a _____ .

    9. He's a _____ .

B. ★ Is _____ your pen?

    ○ Yes, _____ is. Thank _____ .

Practice B

1. Is number five a car? *No, it isn't* .

2. Is number one a TV? _____ .

3. Is number six a radio? _____ .

4. Is number seven a house? _____ .

5. Is number three a bicycle? _____ .

Practice C

1. book ★ *Is this your book* ?

    ○ No, *it isn't* .

2. pencil ★ _____ ?

    ○ Yes, _____ .

3. jacket ★ _____ ?

    ○ No, _____ .

4. car ★ _____ ?

    ○ Yes, _____ .

Practice D

date, in, is, this, very, but, old, address, you, a

1. Is *this* your jacket?

2. My _____ of birth is August 17, 1960.

3. My _____ is 275 Bay Street.

4. New York is a _____ big city.

5. He's _____ my English class.

6. How _____ are you?

7. She _____ sick.

8. I'm not rich, _____ I'm happy.

9. David Benson is _____ teacher.

10. Nice to meet _____ .

Girls, boys . . .

1. It's a beautiful flower.

2. They're beautiful flowers.

3. The park is beautiful, too.

4. She's a happy girl.

5. They're happy girls.

6. The boys are happy, too.

7. a man   men

8. a woman   women

9. a child   children

33

1 flower   2, 3...flower**s**
It is a beautiful flower.
They are beautiful flower**s**.

Dictionary

boy _____   park _____

child _____   the _____

girl _____   woman _____

man _____

Practice A

1. _____ a beautiful flower.

2. _____ beautiful flowers.

3. _____ park is beautiful, too.

4. _____ a happy girl.

5. They're _____ _____ _____ .

6. The boys _____ happy, too.

7. He's a _____ . They're _____ .

8. She's a _____ . They're _____ .

9. He's a _____ . They're _____ .

Practice B

 1 country   2, 3...countr**ies**

1 city   2, 3...cit**ies**

1. It's a new bicycle. *They're new bicycles.*

2. It's a good book. _____

3. She's a doctor. _____

4. He's a poor child. _____

5. It's a small country. _____

6. The rich man is from Mexico. _____
_____

7. She's a beautiful woman. _____
_____

8. It's a big city. _____

9. He's a mechanic. _____

10. The park is beautiful. _____
_____

Practice C

1. tired / teacher / is / English / My
   My English teacher is tired _____ .

2. children / The / poor / are from / city / a big
   _____ .

3. sorry / I'm / but / don't / I / understand
   _____ .

4. country / a small / Japan / is / but / poor / it / isn't
   _____ .

5. students / the / new / from / Are / China
   _____ ?

6. Canada / countries / big / very / are / and the U.S.A.
   _____ .

Family.

A

1980

They are married.

1984

They have a baby.

1. wife
2. husband

3. mother
5. baby
4. father

B

This is Paul Martin and his wife, Elizabeth. They have two children, Rick and Linda.

1. son
2. daughter

3. brother
4. sister

1980   1984

Dictionary

family _____   his _____
have _____   their _____
her _____

Practice A

A. They _____ married.

They _____ a baby.

1. She is his _____ .
2. He is her _____ .
3. She is the _____ .
4. He is the _____ .
5. This is their _____ .

B. This _____ Paul Martin and _____ wife, Elizabeth.

They _____ two children, Rick _____ Linda.

1. He is their _____ .
2. She is their _____ .
3. He is her _____ .
4. She is his _____ .

Practice B

[★ I'm hot.

[★ _Are_ _you_ hot?

[○ Yes, I am.

[★ I'm thirsty, too.

[★ _____ _____ thirsty?

[○ No, I'm not.

[■ Hi.

[○ ★ Hi.

[○ _____ are you, Ken?

[■ _____ so good.

[○ _____ ?

[■ I'm hot.

[○ _____ too.

Practice C

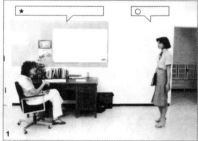

[★ _Are_ _____ a new student?

[○ Pardon?

[★ _____ _____ a new student?

[○ Oh, yes.

[★ _____ _____ _____ from?

[○ Sorry, I don't _____ .

[★ _____ _____ _____ from?

[○ Ahh! I'm from Mexico.

[★ Then, you _____ Spanish.

[○ Yes, but I _____ only a _____ English.

Is he a good baby?

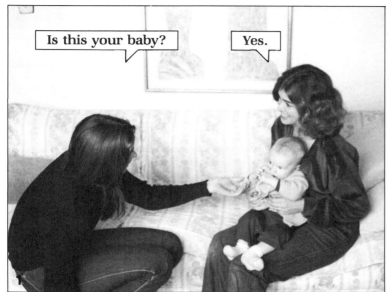

Is he a good baby?
He is <u>not</u> a good baby. |||➡ He isn't a good baby.

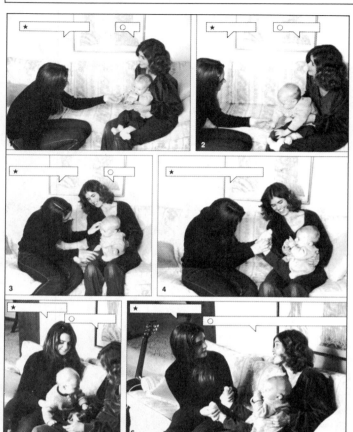

Dictionary

or _____

when _____

Practice A

⎡ ★ _____ _____ your baby?
⎣ ○ Yes.

⎡ ★ Boy _____ girl?
⎣ ○ He's a boy.

⎡ ★ _____ his name?
⎣ ○ Brian.

⎡ ★ Brian. _____ a nice name.

⎡ ★ How old _____ _____ ?
⎣ ○ Nine months.

⎡ ★ _____ _____ a good baby?
⎣ ○ Yes, but he _____ good when he's hungry.

Practice B

 Are they sick?   Yes, they are sick.
    Is she <u>your</u> sister?   Yes, she is <u>my</u> sister.

1. *Is Maria happy* _____ ? Yes, Maria is happy.
2. _____ ? Yes, David is a teacher.
3. _____ ? Yes, today is Monday.
4. _____ ? Yes, the children are tired.
5. _____ ? Yes, this is my book.
6. _____ ? Yes, he is my brother.
7. _____ ? Yes, Miami is a big city.
8. _____ ? Yes, my sister is married.
9. _____ ? Yes, my son is a student.
10. _____ ? Yes, my brothers are students.

Practice C

 They are tired.   No, they are <u>not</u> tired.
    are not |||➡ aren't

1. He is a student. *No, he isn't a student.*
2. She is married. _____
3. Bill is a teacher. _____
4. They are good students. _____
   _____
5. His name is Tom. _____
6. He is a mechanic. _____
7. They are from Italy. _____
8. This month is April. _____
   _____
9. Your baby is hungry. _____
   _____
10. Your husband is a doctor. _____
    _____

What's that?

A

Is this a good book?

Yes, it's OK, but that book is very good.

B

What's that?

Chicken soup.

Is that a chicken sandwich?

Yes, it is.

C

Who's that?

That's Maria. She's a new student.

She's beautiful.

Yes, she is.

this ☞ ■   that ☞ ···· ■
Who is that? ⫸ Who's that?

Dictionary

chicken _____   soup _____

sandwich _____   who _____

Practice A

A. [★ Is _____ a good book?
   [○ Yes, it's OK, but _____ book is very good.

B. [★ _____ that?
   [○ Chicken soup.

   [★ Is _____ a chicken sandwich?
   [○ Yes, _____ is.

C. [★ _____ that?
   [○ That's Maria. _____ a new student.

   [★ _____ beautiful.
   [○ Yes, _____ _____ .

Practice B

1. ☞ ····car   ★ *Is that your car* _____ ?
                    ○ Yes, *it is* _____ .

2. ☞ jacket   ★ _____ ?
                    ○ No, _____ .

3. ☞ English book   ★ _____ ?
                    ○ No, _____ .

4. ☞ ····house   ★ _____ ?
                    ○ Yes, _____ .

Practice C

1. ☞ radio   ★ *What's this* _____ ?
                    ○ *It's a radio* _____ .

2. ☞ ····sandwich   ★ _____ ?
                    ○ _____ .

3. ☞ telephone book ★ _____ ?
                    ○ _____ .

4. ☞ ····pen   ★ _____ ?
                    ○ _____ .

Practice D

What, Who, Where, How

1. _*Who*_____ is that?
2. _____ is she from?
3. _____ are you today?
4. _____ is his name?
5. _____ city is he from?
6. _____ old is your sister?
7. _____ are the new students from?

Practice E

1. *Is he a teacher* _____ ? Yes, he's a teacher.
2. _____ ? No, they aren't students.
3. _____ ? Yes, his name is Brian.
4. _____ ? No, my father isn't a mechanic.
5. _____ ? No, my children aren't sick.
6. _____ ? Yes, they are sisters.

Friends.

1. Is that a photo of you?
   No, it's a photo of my brother and his friends.

2. Can I see?
   Sure.

3. This is my brother Rick and his girlfriend.

4. What's her name?
   Kathy.

5. Who's that?
   That's John. He's Rick's friend.

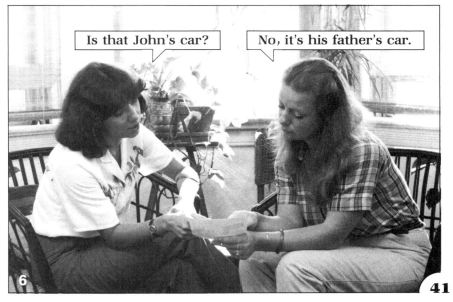

6. Is that John's car?
   No, it's his father's car.

his car her car   John's car

Dictionary

Can I see _____ of _____

friend _____ photo _____

girlfriend _____ sure _____

Practice A

★ Is _____ a photo _____ you?

○ No, it's a photo _____ my brother and
   _____ friends.

★ _____ I see?

○ Sure.

○ This is _____ brother Rick and _____ girlfriend.

★ What's _____ name?

○ Kathy.

★ _____ that?

○ That's John. He's Rick's _____ .

★ Is that _____ car?

○ No, it's his _____ car.

Practice B

1. ★ _What's your daughter's first name_ ?
   ○ My daughter's first name is Anna.

2. ★ _____ ?
   ○ My wife's date of birth is May 6, 1961.

3. ★ _____ ?
   ○ My son's telephone number is 822-4351.

4. ★ _____ ?
   ○ My brother's first name is Brian.

5. ★ _____ ?
   ○ My sister's address is 200 Bay Street.

6. ★ _____ ?
   ○ The teacher's name is David Benson.

7. ★ _____ ?
   ○ My doctor's telephone number is 965-2111.

8. ★ _____ ?
   ○ She's from Mexico.

9. ★ _____ ?
   ○ Her friend's name is Lisa.

10. ★ _____ ?
    ○ That's Kathy.

Practice C

his, her

1. ★ What's your son's name?   ○ _His_ name is
   Brian.

2. ★ What's _____ name?   ○ _____ name is
   Anna.

3. ★ Is that Tony's pen?   ○ Yes, it's _____
   pen.

4. ★ Is that Susan's   ○ Yes, it's _____
   boyfriend?   boyfriend.

Practice D

1. book/Rick
   ★ _Is this your book_ ? ○ _No, it's Rick's book_ .

2. pen/the teacher
   ★ _____ ? ○ _____ .

3. radio/my friend
   ★ _____ ? ○ _____ .

4. dictionary/Susan
   ★ _____ ? ○ _____ .

REVIEW/Lessons 13—18

WHAT NUMBER IS IT?

Number

Number

Number

Number

WHO'S THIS?

1. Who is this? _____
2. How old is she? _____
3. Is this her radio? _____
4. Who is Rick? _____
5. How old is he? _____
6. Is Rick a student? _____

WHAT'S THE CONVERSATION?

★ What's his name?
○ No, he's a mechanic.
★ Is that a photo of your boyfriend?
★ Mike. That's a nice name. Is he a student?
○ No, that's my brother.
○ His name is Mike.

★ *Is that a photo of your boyfriend?* _____
○ _____
★ _____
○ _____
★ _____
○ _____

DISCOVER/Lessons 13–18

Dictionary

parents _____	aunt _____	nephew _____
grandmother _____	uncle _____	sister-in-law _____
grandfather _____	cousin _____	brother-in-law _____
grandparents _____	niece _____	son-in-law _____

Discover A

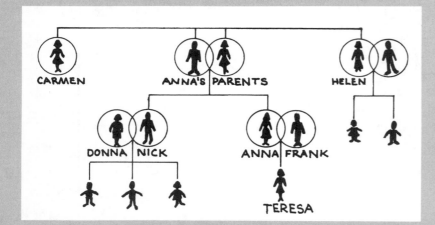

CARMEN   ANNA'S PARENTS   HELEN

DONNA NICK   ANNA FRANK

TERESA

Hello. My name is Anna. I'm married, and I have a daughter. My husband's name is Frank. My daughter's name is Teresa. I have a brother, Nick, and his wife's name is Donna. They have two sons and a daughter. My parents are very happy because they have a big family. My father's sister's name is Carmen. She isn't married, but my mother's sister is married. Her name is Helen. She and her husband have two children. We are a happy family!

1. Donna is Anna's _sister-in-law_ .

2. Nick and Donna's daughter is Anna's _____ .

3. Nick and Donna's sons are Anna's _____ .

4. Frank is Nick's _____ .

5. Frank is Anna's parents' _____ .

6. Anna's mother is Teresa's _____ .

7. Anna's parents are Teresa's _____ .

8. Carmen is Anna's _____ .

9. Helen's husband is Anna's _____ .

10. Helen's children are Anna's _____ .

Discover B

ACROSS

3. My parents have four _____ .
4. Kate and Don are married. She's his _____ .
5. My father's sister is my _____ .
6. My mother's brother is my _____ .
9. My brother is my parents' _____ .
10. I'm Tim's sister. He's my _____ .
11. My nephew's sister is my _____ .
12. My niece is my brother's _____ .

DOWN

1. My parents have a new daughter. She is my new _____ .
2. My daughter's baby boy is my _____ .
3. My aunt's husband is my _____ .
4. Ann is 9 and I'm 7. _____ are children.
7. Tony and Pam are married. He's her _____ .
8. My mother and my father are my _____ .
10. We have four girls and one _____ .

(crossword grid: 3 ACROSS = CHILDREN)

44

Do you have a car?

☞ I have a car.　　Do you have a car?　　I don't have a car.
I do not ⫸ I don't

★ Do you have any children?
○ Yes, I do.
★ How many children do you have?
○ I have three children.

Dictionary

any _____　　how many _____
Good morning. _____

Practice A

[★ Good _____ , David. How _____ you?
[○ Not so good.
[○ I _____ a car.
[○ I _____ a big house.
[○ But I'm _____ happy.
[○ _____ you have a car?
[★ No I _____ .
[○ _____ you have a house?
[★ No, I _____ have a house _____ a car.
[★ But I'm happy.

Practice B

1. car　★ _Do you have a car_ ?
　　○ No, I don't.

2. house　★ _____ ?
　　○ Yes, I do.

3. bicycle　★ _____ ?
　　○ No, _____ _____ .

4. radio　★ _____ ?
　　○ No, I _____ , but I _____ a TV.

5. brother　★ _____ ?
　　○ No, I _____ , but I _____ a sister.

6. daughter　★ _____ ?
　　○ Yes, I _____ , but I _____ have a son.

Practice C

1. children　★ _Do you have any children_ ?
　　○ Yes, _____ .
　　★ How many _____ ?
　　○ _____ .

2. sisters　★ _____ ?
　　○ Yes, _____ .
　　★ How many _____ ?
　　○ _____ .

3. brothers　★ _____ ?
　　○ Yes, I have two brothers.
　　★ Are they in the U.S.A.?
　　○ No, they are in Canada.

4. sisters　★ _____ ?
　　○ Yes, I have one sister.
　　★ _____ _____ in the U.S.A.?
　　○ No, she _____ in Spain.

46

A glass of water.

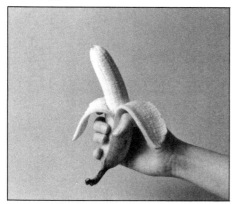

1. a banana

2. an apple

3. an egg

4. an ice cream cone

5. an orange

6. an umbrella

7. a glass

8. a glass of milk

9. a glass of water

10. a cup

11. a cup of tea

12. a cup of coffee

👉 an   a _____
            e _____
            i _____
            o _____
            u _____

Practice A

1. What's number one?   *It's a banana* _____ .
2. What's number two? _____ .
3. What's number three? _____ .
4. What's number four? _____ .
5. What's number five? _____ .
6. What's number six? _____ .
7. What's number seven? _____ .
8. What's number eight? _____ .
9. What's number nine? _____ .
10. What's number ten? _____ .
11. What's number eleven? _____ .
12. What's number twelve? _____ .

Practice B

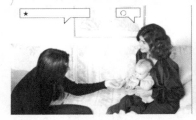 

- ★ _____ _____ your baby?
- ○ Yes.

- ★ Boy _____ girl?
- ○ He's a boy.

- ★ _____ his name?
- ○ Brian.

- ★ Brian. _____ a nice name.

- ★ How old _____ _____ ?
- ○ Nine months.

- ★ _____ _____ a good baby?
- ○ Yes, but he _____ good when he's hungry.

Practice C

- ★ Is _____ a photo _____ you?
- ○ No, it's a photo _____ my brother and _____ friends.

- ★ _____ I see?
- ○ Sure.

- ○ This is _____ brother Rick and _____ girlfriend.

- ★ What's _____ name?
- ○ Kathy.

- ★ _____ that?
- ○ That's John. He's Rick's _____ .

- ★ Is that _____ car?
- ○ No, it's his _____ car.

Can I have . . . ?

A

I'm thirsty. Can I have a glass of water, please?

1

Sure.   Thanks.

2

3

B

Can I have a glass of milk, please?

1

Large or small?

2

Large, please.

3

49

1. a pound of cheese

2. a kilogram of bananas

3. a piece of cake

4. vanilla/chocolate ice cream

Dictionary

Can I . . ? _____   piece _____

chocolate _____   pound _____

kilogram _____   vanilla _____

large _____

Practice A

A. [★ I'm _____ . Can I _____ a glass of water please?

[○ Sure.

[★ _____ .

B. [★ _____ _____ _____ a glass of milk, please?

[○ Large _____ small?

[★ Large, _____ .

Practice B

1. a cup of tea   ★ *Can I have a cup of tea*?
                    ○ *Sure* .

2. an ice cream cone ★ _____ ?
                    ○ Chocolate or vanilla?
                    ★ _____ , please.

3. a sandwich   ★ _____ ?
                    ○ Egg or cheese?
                    ★ _____ , please.

Practice C

Are you . . ?   Do you . . ?

1. happy   *Are you happy* ?
2. car   *Do you have a car* ?
3. TV   _____ ?
4. tired   _____ ?
5. friend   _____ ?
6. married _____ ?

What kind of . . . ?

1

Can I help you?

Yes. What kind of cheese do you have?

2

We have Swiss and Edam.

3

Can I have a pound of Swiss, please?

4

Anything else?

No thanks. That's all.

5

1.　a camera

2.　a watch

Dictionary

all _____　　help _____

American _____　　Japanese _____

anything else _____　　Swiss _____

Canadian _____　　what kind of _____

Practice A

★ Can I _____ you?

○ Yes. What _____ of cheese do you _____ ?

★ We have Swiss _____ Edam.

○ Can I _____ a pound of Swiss, please?

★ Anything else?

○ No, _____ . That's _____ .

Practice B

1. car
★ _What kind of car do you have_ ?
○ I _have_ an American car.

2. TV
★ _____ ?
○ I _____ a Japanese TV.

3. camera
★ _____ ?
○ I have _____ .

4. watch
★ _____ ?
○ I have _____ .

Practice C

1. cheese
★ _What kind of cheese is this_ ?
○ It's Swiss.

2. coffee
★ _____ ?
○ It's Brazilian.

3. cake
★ _____ ?
○ It's chocolate.

4. ice cream
★ _____ ?
○ It's _____ .

Practice D

I, you, he, she, my, your, his, her

1. David is a teacher. _He_ is a good teacher.

2. She is from Canada, but _____ boyfriend is from Brazil.

3. My name is Yoko. _____ am from Japan.

4. _____ is a doctor. Her name is Sharon.

5. Do _____ have a car?

6. He is from Mexico, and _____ wife is from Mexico, too.

7. Do you have a Swiss watch or is _____ watch Japanese?

8. I don't have a Japanese TV. _____ TV is American.

I want . . . .

★ Do you have <u>a car</u>?
○ No, but I want <u>one</u>.

I	want	a car.
Do you	want	a car?
I don't	want	a car.

★ I'm hungry.
○ Do you want an apple?
★ Yes, please.

★ I'm thirsty.
○ Do you want a cup of coffee?
★ No, thanks.

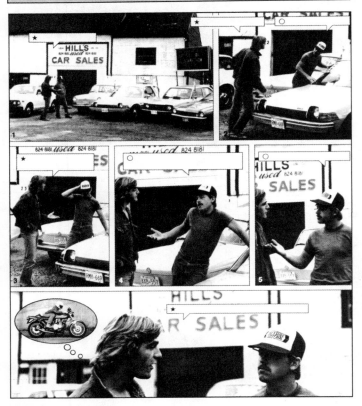

Dictionary

know _____   van _____

maybe _____   want _____

sports car _____

Practice A

[★ _____ a nice car.

[★ Do you _____ a car?
[○ No, but I _____ one.

[★ What kind of car _____ _____ want?

[○ I don't know. _____ a sports car or a van.

[○ What _____ do you want?

[★ I _____ want a car. I want a _____ .

Practice B

1. banana
★ <u>*Do you want a banana*</u> ?
○ No, <u>*thanks*</u> .

2. orange
★ _____ ?
○ Yes, _____ .

3. sandwich
★ _____ ?
○ No, _____ . I'm not hungry.

4. glass of milk ★ _____ ?
○ No, _____ . I'm _____
thirsty.

5. egg
★ _____ ?
○ No, _____ . I'm _____
_____ .

6. cup of tea
★ _____ ?
○ No, thanks, but can I _____
a cup of coffee?

7. _____ ? _____
★ _____ ?
○ No, thanks, but can I have
_____ ?

Practice C

1. car/motorcycle
<u>*I don't want a car. I want a motorcycle*</u> .

2. watch/camera
_____ .

3. small house/big house
_____ .

4. _____ ? _____ / _____ ? _____
_____ .

Practice D

a, an, the, or, but

1. I'm rich <u>*but*</u> I'm not happy.

2. _____ children are tired.

3. Is your baby a boy _____ a girl?

4. I want _____ orange.

5. Can I have _____ banana?

Enough . . .

A

B

Dictionary

enough _____   just a minute _____

hurry up _____   more _____

just a little _____   some _____

Practice A

A. ⎡ ★ Mmm, I want _____ ice cream.
   ⎣ ○ Sure.

   ⎡ ★ _____ up!
   ⎣ ○ Just a _____ .

   ⎡ ★ That's not _____ . I want _____ .
   ⎣ ○ Enough!?

B. ⎡ ★ Do you want _____ tea?
   ⎣ ○ Yes, just a _____ .

   ⎡ ○ That's _____ , thanks.

Practice B

more, enough, little, many

1. ★ Do you want _more_ tea?
   ○ No, thanks.

2. ★ Do you want _____ cake?
   ○ Yes, but just a _____ .

3. ★ Can I have _____ coffee, please?
   ○ Sure.
   ★ Is that _____ ?
   ○ Yes, thank you.

4. ★ Can I have _____ ice cream?
   ○ Sure.
   ○ Is that _____ ?
   ★ No, a _____ more, please.

5. ★ How _____ children do you have?
   ○ Three.
   ★ Do you want _____ children?
   ○ No, three is _____ .

Practice C

┌───┐
│ I want a pound of cheese.   a/an → 1 │
│   I want an orange.   │
│   │
│   I want some cheese.   some → {?}   │
└───┘

a, an, some

1. I want _an_ orange.
2. I want _____ cake.
3. I want _____ piece of cake.
4. I want _____ cup of tea.
5. I want _____ tea.
6. I want _____ milk.
7. Can I have _____ apple?
8. Can I have _____ cup of coffee?
9. Can I have _____ soup?
10. Can I have _____ cheese?
11. Can I have _____ kilogram of bananas?
12. Can I have _____ sandwich?

REVIEW/Lessons 19-24

WHAT IS IT?

apple	baby	camera	car	egg	motorcycle	radio	telephone	watch

1. _____
2. _____
3. _____

4. _____
5. _____
6. _____

7. _____
8. _____
9. _____

WHAT'S THE ANSWER?

1. Betsy is Mark's	wife	daughter
2. She is a	teacher	doctor
3. Mark and Betsy have a	brother	son
4. His name is	Bob	Ben
5. He is	five	four
6. He is a . . . child.	happy	unhappy
7. They live in	Seattle	Toronto
8. They . . . a house.	have	don't have
9. They don't have a	bicycle	car
10. They want a new car this	summer	winter

MATCH THE SENTENCES.

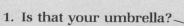

1. Is that your umbrella?
2. I'm hungry.
3. I'm thirsty.
4. Do you want a pound of Edam?
5. Is that your baby daughter?
6. Do you have three sons?
7. Are you hungry?

Do you want a glass of water?
Yes, and a pound of Swiss too, please.
No, but I'm thirsty!
Yes, it is.
Do you want a sandwich?
No, that's my son.
No, only two.

DISCOVER/Lessons 19—24

Dictionary

bread, butter, carrots, corn, fruit, grapes, lemon, orange juice, pepper, salt, sugar, tomato, vegetables

1. fruit

2. _____

3. _____

4. _____

5. _____

6. _____

7. _____

8. _____

13. _____

9. _____

10. _____

11. _____

12. _____

Discover A

1. Corn is a vegetable.
   What else is a vegetable?

   _____
   _____
   _____
   _____

2. A lemon is a fruit.
   What else is a fruit?

   _____
   _____
   _____
   _____

3. Orange juice is a kind of juice.
   What else is a kind of juice?

   _____
   _____
   _____
   _____

Discover B

★ How do you want your coffee?

○ No, thanks. Can I have a small coffee, please?

★ Can I help you?

○ No, that's all.

★ Sorry. No apple juice today, but we have orange and grape juice.

○ Milk, but no sugar.

★ Anything else?

○ Yes, do you have apple juice?

★ Can I help you? _____

○ _____

★ _____

○ _____

★ _____

○ _____

★ _____

○ _____

Discover C

★ Sure. Do you want butter, too?

○ Yes, please.

★ Do you want more salt or maybe some pepper?

○ Very good.

★ How is the soup?

○ No, thanks. The soup is fine, but can I have a piece of bread?

★ How is the soup? _____

○ _____

★ _____

○ _____

★ _____

○ _____

I like . . . .

A

1. I like ice cream.

2. I don't like milk.

Do you like ice cream?

What kind of ice cream do you like?

Do you like milk?

What do you like?

B

I don't like this dress.

Why not?

Because it's old.
I want a new one.

A new dress is expensive.
Do you have enough money?

No, but you do.

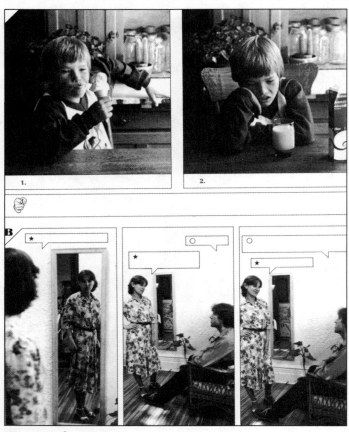

Dictionary

because _____   like _____

dress _____   money _____

expensive _____

Practice A

A. 1. I _____ ice cream.

2. I _____ like milk.

_____ you like ice cream?

What _____ _____ ice cream _____ you like?

_____ you like milk?

What _____ you like?

B. [★ I don't _____ this dress.

[○ Why _____ ?

[★ _____ it's old. I _____ a new one.

[○ A new dress is _____ . Do you _____ enough money?

[★ No, but you do.

Practice B

1. **old, new, do, don't**

    ★ _Do_ you like your jacket?

    ○ No, I _____ .

    ★ Why not?

    ○ Because it's an _____ jacket. I want a _____ one.

2. **I, me, not, don't, isn't**

    ★ Do you like Maria?

    ○ No, I _____ .

    ★ Why _____ ?

    ○ Because she _____ friendly.

    ★ Do you like _____ ?

    ○ Yes, _____ do.

3. **rich, expensive, money**

    ★ I want a new car.

    ○ A new car is _____ .

    ★ That's OK. I have enough _____ . My father is _____ .

Practice C

1. ice cream/vanilla

    ★ _Do you like ice cream_ ?

    ○ _Yes, I do_ .

    ★ _What kind of ice cream do you like_ ?

    ○ _I like vanilla_ .

2. cake/chocolate

    ★ _____ ?

    ○ _____ .

    ★ _____ ?

    ○ _____ .

3. coffee/Mexican

    ★ _____ ?

    ○ _____ .

    ★ _____ ?

    ○ _____ .

4. _____ / _____

    ★ _____ ?

    ○ _____ .

    ★ _____ ?

    ○ _____ .

I need a doctor.

A

B

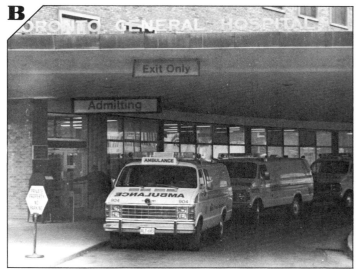

1. When I'm very sick, I go to the hospital.

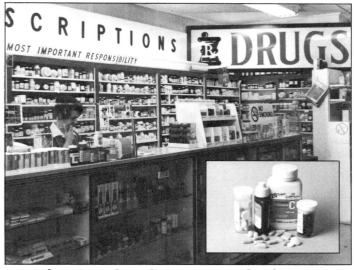

2. When I need medicine, I go to the drugstore.

3. When I need money, I go to the bank.

4. When I need stamps, I go to the post office.

☞ When I need money, I go to the bank. = I go to the bank when I need money.

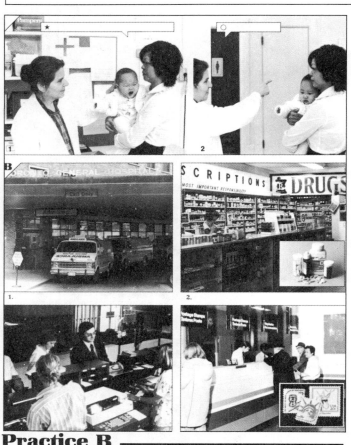

Dictionary

bank _____   need _____

drugstore _____   post office _____

go _____   room _____

hospital _____   stamps _____

medicine _____   to _____

Practice A

A. [★ My baby is very sick. I _____ a doctor.
   [○ _____ to room ten.

B. 1. When I'm very _____ , I go to the _____ .
   2. When I need _____ , I go to the _____ .
   3. When I need _____ , I go to the _____ .
   4. When I need _____ , I go to the _____ .

Practice B

1. _Do you have a car_ ? Yes, I have a car.
2. _____ ? Yes, I speak English.
3. _____ No, I don't understand the teacher.
4. _____ ? No, I don't like Maria.
5. _____ ? No, I don't need a doctor.
6. _____ ? Yes, I want a new TV.

Practice C

go, help, have, need, know, can

★ Can I _help_ you?

○ Yes, I _____ two pounds of coffee.

★ What kind do you want?

○ I don't _____ . What kind do you _____ ?

★ Today we have only Brazilian and Mexican.

○ I want Brazilian, please.

★ Anything else?

○ Yes, _____ I have two stamps, please?

★ Sorry, we don't have stamps. _____ to the post office.

Practice D

☞ Are you rich?   Do you [have] a car?
   I'm not rich   I don't [have] a car.

1. hungry
   Are you hungry ? _No, I'm not hungry_ .

2. want coffee
   Do you want coffee ? _No, I don't want coffee_ .

3. tired
   _____ ? _____ .

4. want a sandwich
   _____ ? _____ .

5. sick
   _____ ? _____ .

6. a student
   _____ ? _____ .

7. married
   _____ ? _____ .

8. have children
   _____ ? _____ .

Where is . . . ?

1. Excuse me. Where is Bay Street?

Go this way three blocks.

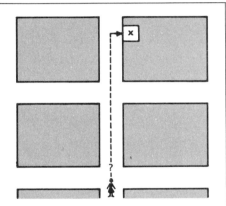

3.
★ Excuse me. Where is the post office?
○ Go this way two blocks. It's on the right.

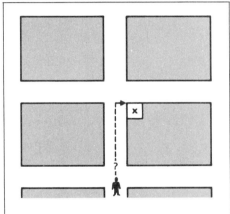

4.
★ Excuse me. Where is the subway?
○ It's on the next corner.

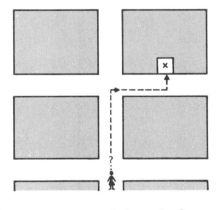

5.
★ Excuse me. Where is the hospital?
○ Go to the next corner. Turn right. It's on the left.

6. Excuse me. Where is King Street?

7. I don't know. Ask the police officer.

8.

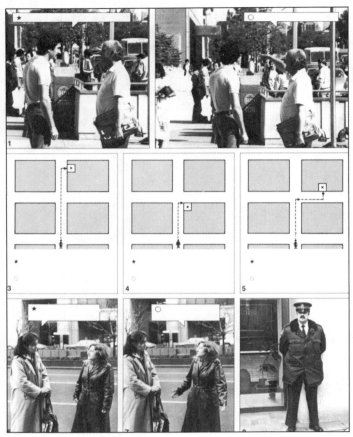

Dictionary

ask _____	on the right _____
block _____	police officer _____
corner _____	subway _____
next _____	turn _____
on the left _____	way _____

Practice A

[★ Excuse me. _____ is Bay Street?
[○ _____ this way three _____ .

[★ Excuse me. _____ is the post office?
[○ _____ this way two _____ . It's _____ the right.

[★ Excuse me. _____ is the subway?
[○ It's on the next _____ .

[★ Excuse me. _____ is the hospital?
[○ Go to the _____ corner. _____ right. It's _____ the left.

[★ Excuse me. _____ is King Street?
[○ I don't know. _____ the police officer.

Practice B

1. Can I have your pen?	185 Bay Street.
2. What's this?	Nineteen.
3. Who's that?	Sure.
4. How are you?	I have two children.
5. How old are you?	It's an English book.
6. What's your address?	That's Tony Santos.
7. What city are you from?	Fine, thanks.
8. How many children do you have?	No, thanks.
9. What kind of camera do you have?	No, he isn't.
10. Do you want a sandwich?	I have a Japanese camera.
11. Is your husband sick?	Yes, they are.
12. Are your friends married?	It's on the next corner
13. Where is the subway?	Tokyo.

Practice C

(i) on, in, to, next

1. The bank is on the _next_ corner.
2. He is _____ my English class.
3. The drugstore is _____ the right.
4. When I'm very sick, I go _____ the hospital.

(ii) of, from, before, after

1. They are _____ China.
2. This is a photo _____ my girlfriend.
3. Tuesday is _____ Monday.
4. June is _____ July.

(iii) and, but, when, because

1. I don't have a car _____ a car is expensive.
2. I understand you, _____ I don't understand the teacher.
3. I speak English, _____ I understand a little Japanese.
4. _____ I need money, I ask my wife.

What time is it?

A

1

2

B

1. It's one o'clock.

2. It's three o'clock.

3. It's six o'clock.

4. It's ten o'clock.

5. It's one thirty.

6. It's two thirty.

7. It's seven thirty.

8. It's eleven thirty.

9. It's quarter after two.   10. It's quarter to four.   11. It's quarter after six.   12. It's quarter to ten.

13. It's twenty after four.   14. It's twenty to five.   15. It's ten after six.   16. It's ten to eight.

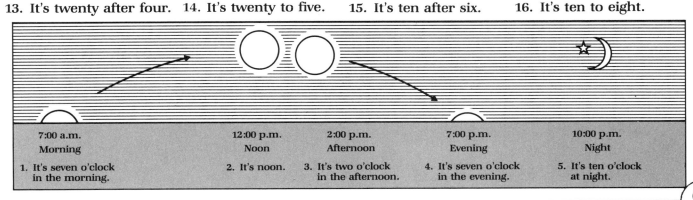

7:00 a.m.	12:00 p.m.	2:00 p.m.	7:00 p.m.	10:00 p.m.
Morning	Noon	Afternoon	Evening	Night

1. It's seven o'clock in the morning.
2. It's noon.
3. It's two o'clock in the afternoon.
4. It's seven o'clock in the evening.
5. It's ten o'clock at night.

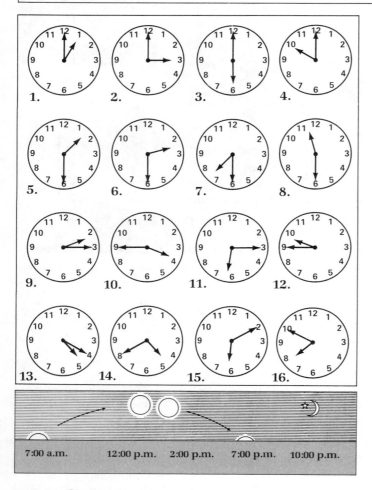

1. 2. 3. 4.

5. 6. 7. 8.

9. 10. 11. 12.

13. 14. 15. 16.

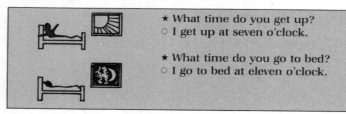

7:00 a.m.   12:00 p.m.   2:00 p.m.   7:00 p.m.   10:00 p.m.

Practice A

A. 1. [★ _____ me. What time _____ _____ ?
       [○ Sorry. I don't _____ a watch.

    2. [★ _____ me. What _____ _____ _____ ?
       [○ It's one _____ .

B. 1. *It's one o'clock.*   2. _____
    3. _____   4. _____
    5. _____   6. _____
    7. _____   8. _____
    9. _____   10. _____
    11. _____   12. _____
    13. _____   14. _____
    15. _____   16. _____

    1. *It's seven o'clock in the morning* _____ .
    2. _____ .
    3. _____ .
    4. _____ .
    5. _____ .

Practice B

★ What time do you get up?
○ I get up at seven o'clock.

★ What time do you go to bed?
○ I go to bed at eleven o'clock.

1. What time do you get up?

   _____ .

2. What time do you go to bed?

   _____ .

3. What time is it?

   _____ .

Practice C

1. ★ Excuse _____ . What time _____ _____ ?
   ○ I _____ know. Ask the teacher.

2. ★ Is it three o'clock?
   ○ No, it's only quarter _____ three.

3. ★ What time do you get _____ ?
   ○ I get up _____ quarter after seven.

4. ★ What time do you go _____ bed?
   ○ I go _____ bed _____ eleven thirty.

Taxi.

I'm a taxi driver. I drive my taxi all day.

In the morning I go to the airport,

the train station,

and the bus station.

In the afternoon I go downtown.

I go to the big hotels.

In the evening I go to the gas station because I need gasoline.

Dictionary

airport _____	hotel _____
bus _____	station _____
downtown _____	taxi _____
drive _____	train _____
gasoline _____	

Practice A

I'm a taxi _____ . I _____ my taxi all day.

In the morning I go to the _____ ,

the _____ station,

and the _____ station.

In the _____ I go _____ .

I go to the big _____ .

In the _____ I go _____ the gas station

because I _____ gasoline.

Practice B

1. 7:00 a.m./airport

   ★ *Where do you go at seven in the morning* ?

   ○ *I go to the airport* .

2. 8:00 a.m./train station

   ★ _____ ?

   ○ _____ .

3. 1:00 p.m./downtown

   ★ _____ ?

   ○ _____ .

4. 7:00 p.m./gas station

   ★ _____ ?

   ○ _____ .

Practice C

1. bank

   ★ *Why do you go to the bank* ?

   ○ *Because I need money* .

2. drugstore ★ _____ ?

   ○ _____ .

3. post office ★ _____ ?

   ○ _____ .

4. gas station ★ _____ ?

   ○ _____ .

Practice D

1. ★ *Excuse me* . *Where is the* train station?

   ○ Go _____ way _____ blocks. It's on the _____ .

2. ★ _____ . _____ bus station?

   ○ Go _____ way _____ block. Turn _____ . It's on the _____ .

I eat a lot.

1. I have breakfast at eight o'clock in the morning. I eat eggs with toast, and I drink two cups of coffee.

2. I have lunch at noon. I eat in a restaurant.

3. I have a snack in the afternoon. I have a sandwich and two glasses of milk.

4. I have a big dinner at home in the evening.

5. At nine o'clock I have another snack.

6. And at night, I dream about food.

☞ I <u>have</u> a sandwich. = I <u>eat</u> a sandwich.
I <u>have</u> a glass of milk. = I <u>drink</u> a glass of milk.
<u>At nine o'clock</u> I have a snack. = I have a snack <u>at nine o'clock</u>.

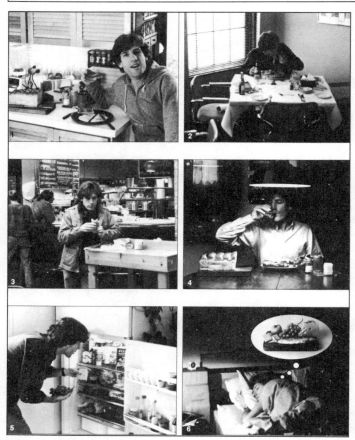

Dictionary

a lot _____	food _____
another _____	home _____
breakfast _____	lunch _____
dinner _____	restaurant _____
dream about_____	snack _____
drink _____	toast _____
eat _____	with _____

Practice A

I have _____ at eight o'clock in the morning.

I _____ eggs with toast, and I _____ two cups of coffee.

I have _____ at noon. I eat in a _____ .

I have a _____ in the afternoon. I have a sandwich and two glasses of milk.

I have a big _____ at _____ in the evening.

At nine o'clock I have _____ snack.

And at night, I dream about _____ .

Practice B

★ What do you have for breakfast?
○ I have two eggs and a cup of tea.

1. ★ What do you have for breakfast?
   ○ _____ .

2. ★ What do you have for lunch?
   ○ _____ .

3. ★ What do you have for dinner?
   ○ _____ .

4. ★ Where do you eat lunch?
   ○ _____ .

5. ★ How many cups of coffee do you drink in the morning?
   ○ _____ .

6. ★ Do you have a snack in the evening?
   ○ _____ .

7. ★ Do you eat a lot?
   ○ _____ .

Practice C

1. get up ★ _*What time do you get up*_ ?
   ○ _*I get up at six thirty*_ .

2. eat lunch ★ _____ ?
   ○ _____ .

3. eat dinner ★ _____ ?
   ○ _____ .

4. go to bed ★ _____ ?
   ○ _____ .

Practice D

to, at, in

1. I eat a snack _____ the evening.

2. I eat dinner _____ home.

3. I eat dinner _____ seven o'clock.

4. I go _____ my class at quarter _____ nine.

5. I go _____ the bank _____ two o'clock _____ the afternoon.

6. I dream about money _____ night.

REVIEW/Lessons 25—30

WHAT'S THE ANSWER?

1. a. Yes, I am.
   b. Yes, I do.

2. a. No, I don't.
   b. I don't have any.

3. a. Yes, they are.
   b. Yes, it is.

4. a. I go to the corner.
   b. It's on the corner.

5. a. I don't know.
   b. No, I don't.

6. a. I have a watch.
   b. It's seven thirty.

7. a. I have a restaurant.
   b. I have a sandwich.

8. a. At eleven p.m.
   b. Because I'm tired.

9. a. No, they aren't.
   b. No, they don't.

YES OR NO?

1. I have dinner in the evening.   YES   NO

2. I eat in a restaurant.   YES   NO

3. I have a small dinner.   YES   NO

4. I eat a large cheese sandwich.   YES   NO

5. I drink a glass of milk.   YES   NO

6. I like to have vanilla ice cream with my cake.   YES   NO

7. I go home at ten o'clock.   YES   NO

8. I have a snack after I go to bed.   YES   NO

9. I eat an apple and some cheese.   YES   NO

10. I like food a lot!   YES   NO

WHAT'S THE WORD?

1. h g u r y n
2. e h e c e s
3. t a s o t
4. y t s i r h t
5. l p e p a
6. c u l n h
7. n d r i e n
8. k a e c
9. c s a k n
10. a w e t r

1. H U N G R Y

DISCOVER/Lessons 25—30

Dictionary

across _____   down _____   past _____

between _____   library _____   school _____

building _____   movie house _____   up _____

department store _____   next to _____   walk _____

Discover A

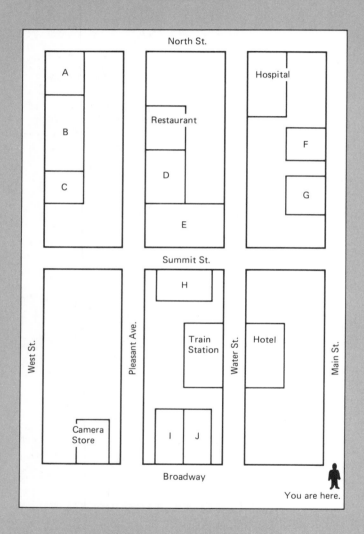

North St.

A

B

C

Restaurant

D

E

Hospital

F

G

Summit St.

H

Train Station

Hotel

Camera Store

I   J

West St.

Pleasant Ave.

Water St.

Main St.

Broadway

You are here.

1. The **library** is on the corner of West Street and North Street.

2. Go down Broadway one block. The **post office** is the first building on the right, just past Water Street.

3. Go up Main Street, past Summit Street. The **drugstore** is on the left, just past the **gas station.**

4. The **school** is on West Street between the **library** and the **book store.**

5. The **bus station** is on Broadway next to the **post office.**

6. Go up Main Street one block. Turn left on Summit Street. Walk two blocks, then turn right on Pleasant Avenue. The **movie house** is the second building on the right, just past the big **department store.**

7. The **bank** is on Summit Street across from the **department store.**

A _library_____   F _____
B _____   G _____
C _____   H _____
D _____   I _____
E _____   J _____

Discover B

1. Where is the hospital?

   It's _____

2. Where is the restaurant?

   It's _____

3. Where is the hotel?

   It's _____

4. Where is the camera store?

   Go _____

   _____

5. Where is the school?

   Go up Main Street _____

Money.

A

1¢
1 cent
a penny

5¢
5 cents
a nickel

10¢
10 cents
a dime

25¢
25 cents
a quarter

$1
a dollar

$10
10 dollars

B

How much is this?

A dollar nineteen.

 98¢

1. Ninety-eight cents.

 $1.98

2. A dollar ninety-eight.

 $2.98

3. Two ninety-eight.

 $3.50/lb.

4. Three fifty a pound.

 $4.25/Kg.

5. Four twenty-five a kilogram.

$235.00

6. Two hundred and thirty-five dollars.

C

I buy oranges at the supermarket. I pay $3.00 for 12 oranges. How much do you pay for oranges?

I buy gasoline at the gas station. I pay $1.40 a gallon. How much do you pay for gasoline?

👉 $2.98   two ninety-eight   = two dollars and ninety eight cents
$3.50/lb.   three fifty a pound   = three dollars and fifty cents for one pound.

Dictionary

buy _____   pay _____

how much _____   supermarket _____

Practice A

A. 1¢   5¢   10¢
   1 _cent_   5 _____   10 _____
   a _penny_   a _____   a _____

   25¢ $1 $10
   25 _____   a _____   10 _____

   a _____

B. ★ How _____ is this?
   ○ A _____ nineteen.
   1. 98¢ _____
   2. $1.98 _____
   3. $2.98 _____
   4. $3.50/lb. _____
   5. $4.25/kg. _____
   6. $235.00 _____

C. 1. I _____ oranges at the _____ .
      I _____ $3.00 _____ twelve oranges.
      How _____ do you _____ for oranges?
   2. I _____ gasoline at the _____ _____ .
      I _____ $1.40 a gallon.
      How much do you _____ for gasoline?

Practice B

1. $1.39   ★ _How much is this_____ ?
            ○ _A dollar thirty-nine_____ .

2. $2.25   ★ _____ ?
            ○ _____ .

3. $345.00 ★ _____ ?
            ○ _____ .

4. $1.69/lb. ★ _____ ?
            ○ _____ .

5. $3.35/kg. ★ _____ ?
            ○ _____ .

Practice D

buy, pay

1. I _____ bananas at the supermarket.
   I _____ eighty-nine cents a pound.
2. I _____ a cup of coffee at the restaurant.
   I _____ fifty cents.
3. I _____ seventy-five cents for an ice cream
   cone. I _____ vanilla.
4. I _____ stamps at the post office. I _____
   thirty-five cents for one stamp.
5. I don't _____ milk because I don't like milk.

Practice C

1. ★ Excuse me. How _____ is this cheese?
   ○ Two fifty a pound.
   ★ Can I _____ three pounds, please?
2. ★ Can I help you?
   ○ Yes, how _____ is this cake?
   ★ Ninety cents a piece.
   ○ Can I _____ three _____ , please?

74

How much is . . . ?

A

B

C

☞ I will ⫸I'll How much <u>is</u> this radio? ☞ ■ this radio ☞ ···· ■ that radio I'll take this <u>book</u>. I'll take <u>it</u>. ⤹

How much <u>are</u> these shoes? these shoes those shoes I'll take these <u>flowers</u>. I'll take <u>them</u>. ⤹

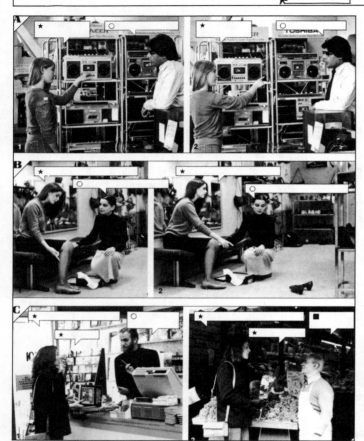

Dictionary

I will (I'll) _____   these _____

take _____   those _____

them _____

Practice A

A. ┌ ★ How much _____ _____ radio?
   └ ○ It's seventy dollars.

   ┌ ★ How much _____ _____ one?
   └ ○ It's ninety dollars.

B. ┌ ★ How much _____ _____ shoes?
   └ ○ They're thirty-five dollars.

   ┌ ★ How much _____ _____ shoes?
   └ ○ They're twenty-nine dollars.

C. ┌ ★ How much _____ this book?
   │ ○ It's two ninety-eight.
   └ ★ I'll take _____ .

   ┌ ★ How much _____ these flowers?
   │ ■ They're three fifty.
   └ ★ I'll take _____ .

Practice B

1. ☞ radio
   $85
   ★ *How much is this radio* ?
   ○ *It's eighty-five dollars* .

2. ☞ ····book
   $4.35
   ★ _____ ?
   ○ _____ .

3. ☞ ····shoes
   $40
   ★ _____ ?
   ○ _____ .

4. ☞ flowers
   $1.99
   ★ _____ ?
   ○ _____ .

5. ☞ dress
   $69.50
   ★ _____ ?
   ○ _____ .

6. ☞ ····apples
   49¢/lb.
   ★ _____ ?
   ○ _____ .

7. ☞ ····watch
   $55
   ★ _____ ?
   ○ _____ .

8. ☞ pens
   75¢
   ★ _____ ?
   ○ _____ .

Practice C

1. umbrella / $20
   ★ *How much is this umbrella* ?
   ○ *It's twenty dollars* .
   ★ *I'll take it* .

2. dress / $18
   ★ _____ ?
   ○ _____ .
   ★ _____ .

3. eggs / $1.15
   ★ _____ ?
   ○ _____ .
   ★ _____ .

4. camera / $82.50
   ★ _____ ?
   ○ _____ .
   ★ _____ .

5. cups / $6.95
   ★ _____ ?
   ○ _____ .
   ★ _____ .

That's too expensive.

110	one hundred and ten
525	five hundred and twenty-five
999	nine hundred and ninety-nine

Dictionary

better _____   price _____

black _____   same _____

both _____   too expensive _____

cheap _____   which _____

color _____   white _____

other _____

Practice A

[★ How _____ is that color TV?

[○ This is a very nice TV. It's eight _____ dollars.

[★ That's _____ expensive _____ me. Do you have a _____ one?

[○ Yes, this one is only six _____ and fifty.

[○ And, I have this one for the same _____ .

[★ Which one is _____ ?

[○ They're both very _____ TVs.

★ Can I help you?
○ Yes, can I see that radio, please?
★ This one?
○ No, the other one.

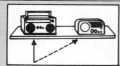

★ Can I help you?
○ Yes, can I see that dress, please?
★ This one?
○ No, the black one.

Practice B

1. ★ Can I help you?

   ○ Yes, I need a new dress.

   ★ This black _____ is very nice. Do you like it?

   ○ Yes, I do. How _____ is it?

   ★ It's one hundred and sixty-five dollars.

   ○ Sorry. That's too _____ for me.

2. ★ How _____ is this camera?

   ○ It's five hundred dollars.

   ★ Do you have a _____ one?

   ○ Yes, this one is only three hundred dollars.

   ★ _____ one is better?

   ○ The one for five hundred dollars is better.

Practice C

1.
   ★ *Can I see that radio, please* ?
   ○ *This one* ?
   ★ *No, the one on the right* .

2.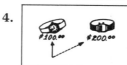
   ★ _____ ?
   ○ _____ ?
   ★ *No, the one for ten dollars* .

3.
   ★ _____ ?
   ○ _____ ?
   ★ _____ .

4.
   ★ _____ ?
   ○ _____ ?
   ★ _____ .

5.
   ★ _____ ?
   ○ _____ ?
   ★ _____ .

6.
   ★ _____ ?
   ○ _____ ?
   ★ _____ .

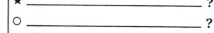

Restaurant.

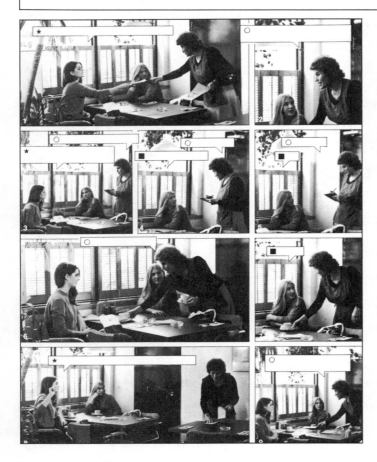

Dictionary

cashier _____	order _____
check _____	ready _____
hamburger _____	special _____
menu _____	tuna fish _____

Practice A

[★ Can I have a _____ , please? Thank you.

[○ Today's _____ is tuna fish sandwich with
  _____ soup.

[○ Are you _____ to order?

  ★ Yes. I want a _____ and a cup of coffee,
  please.

[○ And you?

  ■ _____ coffee, please.

[○ Is that _____ ?

  ■ Yes.

[○ Here _____ your coffees.

[■ Thanks.

[★ Excuse me. Can I have the _____ , please?

[○ Here is your _____ . Please pay the _____ .

Practice B

--MENU--
TODAY'S SPECIAL:
Tuna fish sandwich with vegetable soup $2.25
SANDWICHES
Hamburger 1.50
Hot dog. 90
DESSERTS
Cake. 1.50
Ice cream. 1.00
BEVERAGES
Orange juice . . . . . small .75
large 1.05
Coffee or tea 50

Happy Food Restaurant	
DATE 11/10/85	#2164
1 hamburger	$1.50
1 coffee	.50
TAX 7%	.14
TOTAL	$2.14

1. How much is today's special?

   _____ .

2. How much is a hot dog?

   _____ .

3. Are coffee and tea the same price?

   _____ .

4. Which is cheaper, cake or ice cream?

   _____ .

5. How much is the total check?

   _____ .

6. How many cups of coffee are on the check?

   _____ .

Practice C

(i) **money, price, check, buy, pay**

1. How much is the _____ ?

2. Coffee and tea are the same _____ .

3. Please _____ the cashier.

4. I _____ food at the supermarket.

5. How much _____ do you have in the bank?

(ii) **another, more, enough, a lot**

1. Do you want _____ soup?

2. Do you want _____ piece of cake?

3. That's too expensive. I don't have _____ money.

4. When I'm very hungry, I eat _____ .

(iii) **it, one**

1. This dress is nice. I'll take _____ .

2. I like this TV. How much is _____ ?

3. I don't have a car, but I want _____ .

4. The black dress is beautiful. I want _____ .

I want to go to . . . .

A

1

2

★ Do you go to Dundas Street?

○ No, take bus number seventy-eight.

B

1

2

★ Excuse me. I want to go to the airport. Which bus do I take?

○ Take bus number twelve.

★ Thank you.

C

1

2

★ What time is the next train to Boston?

○ At nine o'clock.

★ How much is a ticket?

○ One way or round trip?

★ Round trip.

○ A round trip ticket is forty-two dollars.

★ Can I have two tickets, please?

D

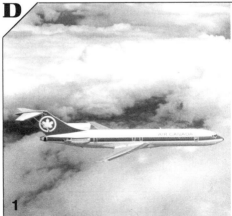

1

2

★ I want to go to Miami. What time is the next flight?

○ Sorry, there is no flight to Miami today. The next one is tomorrow at nine thirty in the morning.

★ Is there a flight tomorrow afternoon?

○ Yes, there is one at twelve twenty.

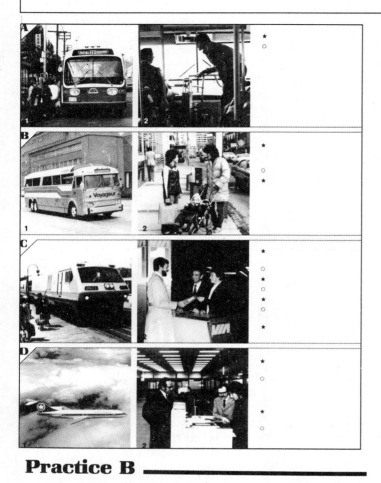

Practice B

1. train/New York/9:00/one way/$98/one ticket
   - ★ *What time is the next train to New York* ?
   - ○ *At nine o'clock* .
   - ★ *How much is a one way ticket* ?
   - ○ *Ninety-eight dollars* .
   - ★ *Can I have one ticket, please* ?

2. bus/Boston/3:00/round trip/$35/four tickets
   - ★ _____ ?
   - ○ _____ .
   - ★ _____ ?
   - ○ _____ .
   - ★ _____ ?

3. flight/Dallas/4:30/one way/$200/one ticket
   - ★ _____ ?
   - ○ _____ .
   - ★ _____ ?
   - ○ _____ .
   - ★ _____ ?

Dictionary

flight _____   there is _____

one way _____   ticket _____

round trip _____   tomorrow _____

Practice A

A. ★ Do you _____ to Dundas Street?
   - ○ No, _____ bus number seventy-eight.

B. ★ Excuse me. I want _____ _____ to the airport. _____ bus do I take?
   - ○ Take bus _____ twelve.
   - ★ Thank you.

C. ★ What time is the _____ train to Boston?
   - ○ _____ nine o'clock.
   - ★ How much is a _____ ?
   - ○ One _____ or round trip?
   - ★ Round trip.
   - ○ A round trip ticket is forty-two dollars.
   - ★ Can I _____ two tickets, please?

D. ✱ I want _____ _____ to Miami. What time is the next _____ ?
   - ○ Sorry, _____ is no flight to Miami today. The next one is _____ at nine thirty in the morning.
   - ★ Is _____ a flight tomorrow afternoon?
   - ○ Yes, _____ is one at twelve twenty.

Practice C

1. Toronto Hospital/#16
   - ★ *Excuse me. I want to go to Toronto Hospital.* .
     Which bus do I take ?
   - ○ *Take bus number sixteen* .
   - ★ *Thank you* .

2. downtown/#60
   - ★ _____ ?
   - ○ _____ .
   - ★ _____ .

82

English is easy.

Do you study English?

Yes, but I can't speak English very well.

English is easy.

Maybe for you, but not for me.

Don't worry. If you try, you can learn English.

I hope so.

can not ▐▐▐➤ can't   I can speak _____ .
                       I can't speak _____ .

★ Can you drive a car?   ★ Can you drive a motorcycle?
○ Yes, I can.   ○ No, I can't.

Dictionary

can _____   learn _____

difficult _____   study _____

easy _____   try _____

if _____   well _____

I hope so _____   worry _____

Practice A

[★ Do you _____ English?
[○ Yes, but I _____ speak English very well.

[★ English is _____ .

[○ Maybe for you, but _____ for me.

[★ Don't _____ . If you try, you can _____
   English.

[○ I _____ so.

Practice B

1. drive a car   ★ _Can you drive a car_ ?
                  ○ No, _I can't_ .

2. speak English ★ _____ ?
                  ○ Yes, _____ .

3. understand me ★ _____ ?
                  ○ Yes, _____ .

4. buy a house   ★ _____ ?
                  ○ No, _____ .

Practice C

can, can't

1. I _____ buy this dress. It's too expensive.

2. I _____ speak Japanese. It's too difficult.

3. I _____ speak English. It's easy.

4. I _____ drive a car. It's easy, too.

5. If you try, you _____ learn Japanese.

6. I _____ buy a car. I don't have enough money.

Practice D

ask, eat, go, speak, worry

1. Don't _____ . You can learn English.

2. Don't _____ this sandwich. It's old.

3. Don't _____ me. I don't know.

4. Don't _____ this way.

5. Don't _____ Spanish in the English class.

Practice E

1. Ask me/the teacher
   Don't ask me. Ask the teacher.

2. Go to New York/Boston
   _____

3. Turn left/right
   _____

4. Buy these shoes/those
   _____

5. Worry today/tomorrow
   _____

REVIEW/Lessons 31-36

WHICH ONE IS IT?

1. a. How much is that?
   b. How much is it?

2. a. They're expensive.
   b. They aren't expensive.

3. a. I'll take it.
   b. I'll take them.

4. a. A dollar nineteen.
   b. A dollar ninety.

5. a. It's thirteen dollars.
   b. It's thirty dollars.

6. a. Two fifteen a pound.
   b. Two fifty a pound.

7. a. There's a flight today.
   b. There isn't a flight today.

8. a. Do you want to go?
   b. Don't you want to go?

9. a. I can help you.
   b. I can't help you.

WHAT NUMBER IS IT?

WHAT'S THE CONVERSATION?

★ An evening flight, please.

○ One way to Chicago on Flight 104. That's $90. Have a nice flight.

○ Do you want a morning or an evening flight?

★ I want to go to Chicago on June 16.

★ That's fine. I want a one way ticket, please.

★ Thank you.

○ Flight 104 is at 6:30 p.m. on June 16. Is that flight OK?

★ *I want to go to Chicago on June 16.*
○ _____
★ _____
○ _____
★ _____
○ _____
★ _____

85

DISCOVER/Lessons 31–36

Dictionary

bakery _____	film _____	key _____
boots _____	furniture store _____	paint _____
cassette player _____	gloves _____	tools _____
clothing store _____	hardware store _____	Do you have change? _____
electronics store _____	jewelry store _____	a twenty dollar bill _____

Discover A

Where can you buy it?

1. a bookcase *At a furniture store* _____
2. a jacket _____
3. a cassette player _____
4. a watch _____
5. paint _____

Where can you buy them?

6. gloves _____
7. keys _____
8. chairs _____
9. cakes _____
10. tools _____

Discover B

a bed, a dictionary, a dress, a ticket, a TV,
a sandwich, bread, film, medicine, boots

1. I can buy _____ at the shoe store.
2. I can buy _____ at the camera store.
3. I can buy _____ at the book store.
4. I can buy _____ at the bus station.
5. I can buy _____ at the clothing store.
6. I can buy _____ at the bakery.
7. I can buy _____ at the furniture store.
8. I can buy _____ at the restaurant.
9. I can buy _____ at the electronics store.
10. I can buy _____ at the drugstore.

Discover C

1. What can you buy at a hardware store?

_____ _____

_____ _____

2. What can you buy at a furniture store?

_____ _____

_____ _____

3. What can you buy at a clothing store?

_____ _____

_____ _____

4. What can you buy at an electronics store?

_____ _____

_____ _____

Discover D

★ Excuse me. Do you have change for a twenty dollar bill?
○ Sure. I have a ten and two fives. Is that OK?
★ That's fine. Thank you very much.

1. a ten dollar bill

★ *Excuse me. Do you have change*
for a ten dollar bill? _____
○ _____
★ _____

2. a dollar

★ _____
_____
○ _____
_____
★ _____

3. a quarter

★ _____
_____
○ _____
_____
★ _____

86

WORD LIST

a 9
a lot 70
about 69
address 27
after 25
afternoon 65
airport 67
all 51
am 9
American 52
an 47
and 3
another 69
any 46
anything else 51
apple 47
April 25
are 3
ask 64
at 66
August 25

baby 35
bag 31
banana 47
bank 61
beautiful 23
because 59
bed 66
before 25
better 77
beverage 80
bicycle 31
big 23
birth 27
black 78
block 63
book 13
both 77
boy 33
Brazilian 52
breakfast 69
brother 35
bus 67
but 21
buy 73
bye 7

cake 50
can 41
Canadian 52
can't 83
car 31
cashier 79
cent 73
cheap 78
cheaper 77
check 79
cheese 50
cheeseburger 80
chicken 39
child 33
children 33
chocolate 50
city 23
class 9
coffee 47
cold 17
color 77
corner 63
country 23
cup 47

date 27
daughter 35
day 25
December 25
dessert 80
difficult 84
dime 73
dinner 69

do 45
doctor 31
dollar 73
don't 21
downtown 67
dream 69
dress 59
drink 69
drive 67
driver 67
drugstore 61

easy 83
eat 69
egg 47
else 51
English 9
enough 55
evening 65
excuse 13
expensive 59

fall 25
family 36
father 35
February 25
fine 3
first 2
flight 81
flower 33
food 69
for 73
Friday 25
friend 41
from 21

gallon 73
gas station 67
gasoline 67
get up 66
girl 33
girlfriend 41
glass 47
go 61
good 7
good morning 45
good-bye 7

hamburger 79
happy 17
have 35
he 9
hello 2
help 51
her 36
here 5
he's 11
hi 7
his 35
home 69
hope 83
hospital 61
hot 17
hot dog 80
hotel 67
house 31
how 3
how many 46
hungry 17
hurry up 55
husband 35

I 9
ice cream 55
ice cream cone 47
if 83
I'll 75
I'm 11
in 9
is 2

isn't 23
it 31
it's 31

jacket 31
January 25
Japanese 52
juice 80
July 25
June 25
just 55

kilogram 50
kind 51
know 53

large 49
last 2
learn 83
left 63
like 59
little 21
lot 69
lunch 69

man 33
many 46
March 25
married 17
May 25
maybe 53
me 13
mechanic 31
medicine 61
meet 7
men 33
menu 79
milk 47
minute 55
Miss 8
Monday 25
money 59
month 25
more 55
morning 45
mother 35
motorcycle 53
Mr. 8
Mrs. 8
Ms. 8
much 73
my 2

name 2
need 61
new 21
next 63
nice 7
nickel 73
night 65
no 19
noon 65
not 19
November 25
number 27

o'clock 65
October 25
of 27
oh 13
OK 13
old 27
on 64
one 11
one way 81
only 21
or 37
orange 47
order 79
other 77

pardon 5
park 33
pay 73
pen 14
penny 73
photo 41
piece 50
please 5
police officer 63
poor 24
post office 61
pound 50
price 77

quarter 73

radio 31
ready 79
restaurant 69
return 81
rich 24
right 63
room 61

same 77
sandwich 39
Saturday 25
see 41
September 25
she 9
she's 11
shoes 75
sick 17
sign 5
signature 2
sister 36
small 23
snack 69
so 19
some 55
son 35
sorry 13
soup 39
Spanish 21
speak 21
special 79
spell 5
sports car 53
spring 25
stamp 61
station 67
street 27
student 9
study 83
subway 63
summer 25
Sunday 25
supermarket 73
sure 41
Swiss 51

take 75
taxi 67
taxi driver 67
tea 47
teacher 9
telephone 14
television 31
thank you 5
thanks 3
that 14
that's 13
the 33
their 36
them 75
then 21
there 81
these 75
they 9
they're 11

thirsty 17
this 7
those 75
Thursday 25
ticket 81
time 65
tired 17
to 7
toast 69
today 25
tomorrow 81
too 7
train 67
try 83
Tuesday 25
tuna fish 79
turn 63
TV 31

umbrella 47
understand 21
unhappy 17
up 5

van 53
vanilla 50
vegetable 79
very 9

want 53
watch 65
water 47
way 63
we 9
Wednesday 25
week 25
welcome 5
well 83
we're 11
what 23
what's 2
when 37
where 21
which 77
white 78
who 40
who's 39
why 19
wife 35
will 76
winter 25
with 69
woman 33
women 33
worry 83

year 25
yes 9
you 3
your 2
you're 5

ANSWER KEY

Lesson 1, page 4
Practice C
1. name, is, are, thanks, you
2. first, last

Lesson 2, page 6
Practice C
2. How are you?
3. Spell your last name, please.
4. Spell your first name, please.
5. Thank you.

Lesson 3, page 8
Practice B
1. your, please, Thank, welcome
2. is, you, you, too
3. How, Fine, And, Fine
Practice C
1. Spell your last name.
2. Nice to meet you.
3. My last name is Benson.
4. How are you?
5. What's your last name?
Listening Activity
A. 1. nice 2. welcome 3. your
   4. thanks 5. first 6. please
B. 1. b 2. a 3. a 4. a 5. a

Lesson 4, page 10
Practice B
1. We   4. She   7. He
2. They   5. We   8. I
3. He   6. They   9. You
Practice C
1. is   5. are   9. is   13. are
2. am   6. are   10. is   14. are
3. are   7. is   11. are 15. is
4. is   8. are   12. am   16. are

Lesson 5, page 12
Practice B
I'm, He's, She's, They're, We're,
You're, you're
Practice C
2. We're students.
3. You're welcome.
4. He's in my English class.
5. She's in my English class, too.
6. What's your name?
7. They're teachers.
8. I'm a student.
9. They're very good students.

Lesson 6, page 14
Practice C
1. You're   5. your
2. you   6. you
3. You're   7. you
4. your   8. You're

REVIEW: Lessons 1–6, page 15
What's the Word?
1. this   4. your   7. they're
2. am   5. we're 8. my
3. she   6. hi   9. Mrs.
Yes or No?
1. yes   3. no   5. no   7. yes
2. no   4. yes 6. yes 8. yes
What's One + One?
Across 1. two 3. thirty 8. seventeen
10. forty 11. eleven 12. he's 13. you're
Down 2. one 3. twelve 4. twenty
5. they're 6. three 7. eight 8. she's
9. ten 10. four

DISCOVER: Lessons 1–6, page 16
Discover A
1. paper   4. bookcase
2. desk   5. chair
3. plant   6. lamp
Discover B
1. bookcase   5. telephone
2. plant   6. stapler
3. lamp   7. paper
4. chair   8. desk

Lesson 8, page 20
Practice B
2. Are you hot?
   Yes, I am./No, I'm not.
3. Are you cold?
4. Are you happy?
5. Are you married?
6. Are you sick?

Practice C
(i) 1. They are hot.
    2. He is unhappy.
    3. She is thirsty.
    4. We are married.
(ii)
1. is   3. am   5. are   7. Are
2. is   4. are 6. is
(iii)
1. My   3. I   5. My   7. My
2. me   4. Me   6. I

Lesson 9, page 22
Practice B
1. Tony.   4. Canada.
2. A telephone.   5. Yes, I am.
3. Fine.   6. Santos.
Practice C
1. Nice   4. don't   7. me
2. What's 5. speak   8. from
3. not   6. Where
Practice D
2. Are you married? Yes, I'm
   married./No, I'm not married.
3. Are you a teacher? Yes, I'm a
   teacher./No, I'm not a teacher.
4. Are you from Japan? Yes, I'm
   from Japan./No, I'm not from
   Japan.
5. Are you a new student? Yes, I'm
   a new student./No, I'm not a
   new student.
6. Are you hungry? Yes, I'm
   hungry./No, I'm not hungry.
Listening Activity
A. 1. she, he. 2. you, your
   3. student, students 4. me, my
   5. what, hot 6. that, last
B. 1. yes 2. no 3. yes
   4. no 5. no 6. yes

Lesson 10, page 24
Practice B
2. Where are you from?
3. What city are you from?
4. How are you?
5. Are you hot?
Practice C
1. isn't   3. isn't   5. is
2. is   4. isn't
Practice D
2. Canada isn't a poor country.
3. Switzerland is small.
4. New York is a big city.
5. Alaska is very cold.
6. Paris is a beautiful city.
7. Tokyo is a very big city.
8. Brazil isn't cold.

Lesson 11, page 26
Practice B
1. Tuesday   7. Saturday
2. Monday   8. Thursday
3. January   9. November
4. July

Lesson 12, page 28
Practice B
2. What's your telephone number?
3. How old are you?
4. What's your date of birth?
5. Where are you from?
6. Are you married?
7. What city are you from?
8. How are you?
9. What's your name?
10. Are you tired?
Practice C
1. Today   4. little   7. speak
2. don't   5. country   8. city
3. not   6. me   9. from

REVIEW: Lessons 7–12, page 29
How Are You?
2. She is thirsty.
3. They are happy.
4. I am tired.
5. We are cold.
6. You are sick.
Kim Tanaka
1. No   3. No   5. Yes   7. Yes
2. Yes   4. Yes 6. No

DISCOVER: Lessons 7–12, page 30
Discover A
2. Eight forty-nine West University
   Street, Apartment fourteen fifty
3. Seven thirty-four South Main
   Avenue, Albany
4. Thirty-five eighteen North
   Orange Drive, Los Angeles
5. Sixty-two Washington Place,
   Apartment twenty-eight thirty-
   two
Discover B
2. October twenty-seventh,
   nineteen fifty-nine
3. November third, nineteen sixty-
   four
4. June first, nineteen thirty-five
Discover C
2. 428-5000
3. 341-3059

Lesson 13, page 32
Practice B
2. Yes, it is.   4. Yes, it is.
3. No, it isn't.   5. No, it isn't.
Practice D
1. this   4. very   7. is   10. you
2. date   5. in   8. but
3. address 6. old   9. a

Lesson 14, page 34
Practice B
2. They're good books.
3. They're doctors.
4. They're poor children.
5. They're small countries.
6. The rich men are from Mexico.
7. They're beautiful women.
8. They're big cities.
9. They're mechanics.
10. The parks are beautiful.
Practice C
2. The poor children are from a big
   city.
3. I'm sorry, but I don't
   understand.
4. Japan is a small country, but it
   isn't poor.
5. Are the new students from
   China?
6. Canada and the U.S.A. are very
   big countries.

Lesson 15, page 36
Listening Activity
A. 1. big, bad 2. men, man
   3. street, speak 4. new, no
   5. here, where 6. women, woman
B. 1. yes 2. no 3. no 4. no 5. yes 6. no

Lesson 16, page 38
Practice B
2. Is David a teacher?
3. Is today Monday?
4. Are the children tired?
5. Is this your book?
6. Is he your brother?
7. Is Miami a big city?
8. Is your sister married?
9. Is your son a student?
10. Are your brothers students?
Practice C
2. No, she isn't married.
3. No, Bill isn't a teacher.
4. No, they aren't good students.
5. No, his name isn't Tom.
6. No, he isn't a mechanic.
7. No, they aren't from Italy.
8. No, this month isn't April.
9. No, my baby isn't hungry.
10. No, my husband isn't a doctor.

Lesson 17, page 40
Practice B
2. Is this your jacket? No, it isn't.
3. Is this your English book?
4. Is that your house?
Practice C
1. What's this? It's a radio.
2. What's that? It's a sandwich.
3. What's this? It's a telephone
   book.

4. What's that? It's a pen.
Practice D
1. Who   4. What   6. How
2. Where   5. What   7. Where
3. How
Practice E
2. Are they students?
3. Is his name Brian?
4. Is your father a mechanic?
5. Are your children sick?
6. Are they sisters?

Lesson 18, page 42
Practice B
2. What's your wife's date of
   birth?
3. What's your son's telephone
   number?
4. What's your brother's first
   name?
5. What's your sister's address?
6. What's the teacher's name?
7. What's your doctor's telephone
   number?
8. Where is she from?
9. What's her friend's name?
10. Who's that?
Practice C
1. His   3. his, His   5. her
2. her, Her 4. his
Practice D
1. Is this your book? No, it's Rick's
   book.
2. Is this your pen? No, it's the
   teacher's pen.
3. No, it's my friend's radio.
4. No, it's Susan's dictionary.

REVIEW: Lessons 13–18, page 43
What Number Is it?
3   2
1   4

Who's This? (Accept similar
answers.)
1. This is Kathy Jackson.
2. She's 13.
3. No, it isn't.
4. He's Kathy's brother.
5. He's 21.
6. No, he isn't.
What's the Conversation?
★ Is that a photo of your boyfriend?
○ No, that's my brother.
★ What's his name?
○ His name is Mike.
★ Mike. That's a nice name. Is he a
  student?
○ No, he's a mechanic.

DISCOVER: Lessons 13–18, page 44
Discover A
1. sister-in-law   6. grandmother
2. niece   7. grandparents
3. nephews   8. aunt
4. brother-in-law   9. uncle
5. son-in-law   10. cousins
Discover B
Across 3. children 4. wife 5. aunt
6. uncle 9. son 10. brother 11. niece
12. daughter
Down 1. sister 2. grandson 3. cousin
4. we 7. husband 8. parents 10. boy

Lesson 19, page 46
Practice B
2. Do you have a house?
3. Do you have a bicycle? I don't.
4. Do you have a radio? don't, have
5. Do you have a brother? don't,
   have
6. Do you have a daughter? do,
   don't
Practice C
1. Yes, I do.
   How many children do you
   have?
   I have . . . child/children.
2. Do you have any sisters?
   Yes, I do.
   How many sisters do you have?
3. Do you have any brothers?
4. Do you have any sisters?
   Is she, is

Lesson 21, page 50
Practice B
2. Can I have an ice cream cone? Chocolate/Vanilla
3. Can I have a sandwich? Egg/Cheese

Practice C
3. Do you have a TV?
4. Are you tired?
5. Do you have a friend?
6. Are you married?

Listening Activity
A. 1. when, where 2. or, old 3. who, how 4. her, are 5. his, this 6. egg, eight
B. 1. a 2. b 3. b 4. a 5. b 6. b 7. a 8. b

Lesson 22, page 52
Practice D
1. He   3. I   5. you   7. your
2. her   4. She   6. his   8. My

Lesson 23, page 54
Practice B
2. Do you want an orange? Yes, please.
3. Do you want a sandwich? thanks
4. Do you want a glass of milk? thanks, not
5. Do you want an egg? thanks, not hungry
6. Do you want a cup of tea? have

Practice D
1. but   3. or   5. a
2. The   4. an

Lesson 24, page 56
Practice B
1. more   4. more, enough,
2. more, little   little
3. more,   5. many, more,
enough   enough

Practice C
1. an   4. a   7. an   10. some
2. some   5. some   8. a   11. a
3. a   6. some   9. some   12. a

REVIEW: Lessons 19–24, page 57
What Is It?
1. It's a car.   5. It's a camera.
2. It's a baby.   6. It's a motorcycle.
3. It's a   7. It's an egg.
telephone.   8. It's a radio.
4. It's an   9. It's a watch.
apple.

What's the Answer?
1. wife   5. four   8. have
2. doctor   6. happy   9. car
3. son   7. Seattle   10. winter
4. Ben

Match the Sentences.
1. Yes, it is.
2. Do you want a sandwich?
3. Do you want a glass of water?
4. Yes, and a pound of Swiss, too, please.
5. No, that's my son.
6. No, only two.
7. No, but I'm thirsty!

DISCOVER: Lessons 19–24, page 58
Discover B
★ Can I help you?
○ Yes, do you have apple juice?
★ Sorry. No apple juice today, but we have orange and grape juice.
○ No, thanks. Can I have a small coffee?
★ How do you want your coffee?
○ Milk, but no sugar.
★ Anything else?
○ No, thanks.

Discover C
★ How is the soup?
○ Very good.
★ Do you want more salt or maybe some pepper?
○ No, thanks. The soup is fine, but can I have a piece of bread?
★ Sure. Do you want butter, too?
○ Yes, please.

Lesson 25, page 60
Practice B
1. Do, don't, old, new

2. don't, not, isn't, me, I
3. expensive, money, rich

Lesson 26, page 62
Practice B
2. Do you speak English?
3. Do you understand the teacher?
4. Do you like Maria?
5. Do you need a doctor?
6. Do you want a new TV?

Practice C
help, need, know, have, can, Go

Practice D
3. Are you tired?
4. Do you want a sandwich?
5. Are you sick?
6. Are you a student?
7. Are you married?
8. Do you have children?

Lesson 27, page 64
Practice B
1. Sure.
2. It's an English book.
3. That's Tony Santos.
4. Fine, thanks.
5. Nineteen.
6. 185 Bay Street.
7. Tokyo.
8. I have two children.
9. I have a Japanese camera.
10. No, thanks.
11. No, he isn't.
12. Yes, they are.
13. It's on the next corner.

Practice C
(i) 1. next 2. in 3. on 4. to
(ii) 1. from 2. of 3. after 4. before
(iii) 1. because 2. but 3. and 4. When

Listening Activity
A. 1. b 2. a 3. b 4. b 5. b 6. a
B. 1. b 2. a 3. a 4. a 5. b 6. a

Lesson 28, page 66
Practice C
1. me, is it, don't   3. up, at
2. to   4. to, to, at

Lesson 29, page 68
Practice B
2. Where do you go at eight in the morning? I go to the train station.
3. Where do you go at one in the afternoon? I go downtown.
4. Where do you go at seven in the evening? I go to the gas station.

Practice C
2. ○ Because I need medicine.
3. ○ Because I need stamps.
4. ○ Because I need money.

Practice D
1. Excuse me. Where is the this, two, left
2. Excuse me. Where is the this, one, left, right

Lesson 30, page 70
Practice D
1. in   3. at   5. to, at, in
2. at   4. to, to, at

REVIEW: Lessons 25–30, page 71
What's the Answer?
1. b   4. b   7. b
2. a   5. a   8. b
3. b   6. b   9. a

Yes or No?
1. Yes   5. Yes   8. No
2. Yes   6. No   9. Yes
3. No   7. No   10. Yes
4. No

What's the Word?
1. hungry   5. apple   8. cake
2. cheese   6. lunch   9. snack
3. toast   7. dinner   10. water
4. thirsty

DISCOVER: Lessons 25–30, page 72
Discover A
A. library   F. drugstore
B. school   G. gas station
C. book store   H. bank
D. movie house   I. bus station
E. department   J. post office
store

Discover B (Accept similar answers.)
1. It's on the corner of Water Street and North Street.
2. It's on Pleasant Street, just past the movie house.
3. It's on Water Street across from the train station.
4. Go down Broadway two blocks. The camera store is on the right, just past Pleasant Avenue.
5. Go up Main Street one block. Turn left on Summit Street. Walk three blocks, then turn right on West Street. The school is on the right, between the library and the book store.

Lesson 31, page 74
Practice B
2. Two twenty-five.
3. Three hundred and forty-five dollars.
4. A dollar sixty-nine a pound.
5. Three thirty-five a kilogram.

Practice C
1. much, have
2. much, have, pieces

Practice D
1. buy, pay   4. buy, pay
2. buy, pay   5. buy
3. pay, buy

Lesson 32, page 76
Practice B
2. How much is that book? It's four thirty-five.
3. How much are those shoes? They're forty dollars.
4. How much are these flowers? They're a dollar ninety-nine.
5. How much is this dress? It's sixty-nine dollars and fifty cents.
6. How much are those apples? They're forty-nine cents a pound.
7. How much is that watch? It's fifty-five dollars.
8. How much are these pens? They're seventy-five cents.

Practice C
2. How much is this dress? It's eighteen dollars. I'll take it.
3. How much are these eggs? They're a dollar fifteen. I'll take them.
4. How much is this camera? It's eighty-two fifty. I'll take it.
5. How much are these cups? They're six ninety-five. I'll take them.

Lesson 33, page 78
Practice B
1. one, much, expensive
2. much, cheaper, Which

Practice C (sample answers)
2. Can I see that book, please? This one?
3. Can I see that dress, please? This one? No, the white one.
4. Can I see that watch, please? This one? No, the one for two hundred dollars.
5. Can I see that pen, please? This one? No, the other one.
6. Can I see that umbrella, please? This one? No, the one on the left.

Listening Activity
A. 1. At the post office 2. At a bank 3. At a gas station 4. At a hotel 5. At a restaurant
B. 1. 595-3876 2. $89.95 3. The black dress is cheaper.

Lesson 34, page 80
Practice B
1. Two twenty-five.
2. Ninety cents.
3. Yes, they are.

4. Ice cream is cheaper.
5. Two sixty-eight.
6. Two cups.

Practice C
(i) 1. check   3. pay   5. money
2. price   4. buy
(ii) 1. more   3. enough
2. another   4. a lot
(iii) 1. it   2. it   3. one   4. one

Lesson 35, page 82
Practice B
2. ★ What time is the next bus to Boston?
○ At three o'clock.
★ How much is a round trip ticket?
○ Thirty-five dollars.
★ Can I have four tickets, please?
3. ★ What time is the next flight to Dallas?
○ At four thirty.
★ How much is a one way ticket?
○ Two hundred dollars.
★ Can I have one ticket, please?

Lesson 36, page 84
Practice B
2. Can you speak English? Yes, I can.
3. Can you understand me?
4. Can you buy a house?

Practice C
1. can't   3. can   5. can
2. can't   4. can   6. can't

Practice D
1. worry   3. ask   5. speak
2. eat   4. go

Practice E
2. Don't go to New York. Go to Boston.
3. Don't turn left. Turn right.
4. Don't buy these shoes. Buy those shoes.
5. Don't worry today. Worry tomorrow.

REVIEW: Lessons 31–36, page 85
Which One Is It?
1. a   4. a   7. b
2. b   5. b   8. a
3. b   6. b   9. b

What Number Is It?
4   2
1   3

What's the Conversation?
★ I want to go to Chicago on June 16.
○ Do you want a morning or an evening flight?
★ An evening flight, please.
○ Flight 104 is at 6:30 p.m. on June 16. Is that flight OK?
★ That's fine. I want a one way ticket, please.
○ One way to Chicago on Flight 104. That's $90. Have a nice flight.
★ Thank you.

DISCOVER: Lessons 31–36, page 86
Discover A
1. At a furniture store.
2. At a clothing store.
3. At an electronics store.
4. At a jewelry store.
5. At a hardware store.
6. At a clothing store.
7. At a hardware store.
8. At a furniture store.
9. At a bakery.
10. At a hardware store.

Discover B
1. boots   6. bread
2. film   7. a bed
3. a dictionary   8. a sandwich
4. a ticket   9. a TV
5. a dress   10. medicine

Discover D (sample answers)
1. Sure. I have a five and five ones.
2. Sure. I have three quarters, two dimes and a nickel.
3. Sure. I have a dime, two nickels, and five pennies.

SKILLS INDEX